MW01633654

BLUEPRINT FOR IMMORTALITY

Harold Saxton Burr, Ph.D

E. K. Hunt Professor Emeritus, Anatomy
Yale University School of Medicine

Portrait by Artzybasheff. Reproduced by permission of Yale University Art Gallery
Portrait was gift of former students, alumni and colleagues of Yale University School of Medicine

HAROLD SAXTON BURR

Blueprint for Immortality

The Electric Patterns of Life

LONDON

NEVILLE SPEARMAN

First published in Great Britain 1972
by Neville Spearman Limited
112 Whitfield Street, London W1P 6DP

SBN 85435 281 3

Library of Congress Catalog Card Number
72-75971

Set in 11 pt Juliana, 1½ pt leaded, and
printed by Northumberland Press Ltd, Gates-
head. Bound by Mansell Bookbinders Ltd.
London

CONTENTS

ILLUSTRATIONS

FOREWORD

The Universe in which we find ourselves and from which we can not be separated is a place of Law and Order. It is not an accident, nor chaos. It is organized and maintained by an Electro-dynamic Field capable of determining the position and movement of all charged particles.

For nearly half a century the logical consequences of this theory have been subjected to rigorously controlled experimental conditions and met with no contradictions.

H. S. Burr

PART I

Voyage of Discovery

CHAPTER ONE
An Adventure in Science

1

We live in troubled and difficult times. There are wars and dangers of war. In many parts of the world there are revolts, protests, crime and lawlessness in ceaseless eruption. And over this age hangs the Sword of Damocles of possible nuclear destruction.

More and more people ask themselves despondently whether life has any sense or purpose. Many are tempted to believe that man is an accident, left to grapple with his lonely fate on an insignificant planet in a harsh and lawless Universe.

In a materialistic, scientific age many find it hard to accept those religious beliefs that sustained their forefathers in times which—to them—seemed as troubled and perilous as the present. They would like to believe that man is no accident and that the Universe in which he lives is one of law, order and purpose. But, dazzled by the methods and triumphs of science, they are unwilling to take anything on trust; they demand some 'scientific' proof or evidence.

Until some forty years ago this demand could not be met because the necessary electronic instruments and techniques had not been developed. When these became available, however, an entirely new approach to the nature of man and his place in the Universe became possible. For these instruments revealed that man—and, in fact, *all forms*—are ordered and controlled by electro-dynamic fields which can be measured and mapped with precision.

Though almost inconceivably complicated, the 'fields of life' are of the same nature as the simpler fields known to modern physics and obedient to the same laws. Like the fields of physics, they are a part of the organization of the Universe and are influenced by the vast forces of space. Like the fields of physics, too, they have organizing and directing qualities which have been revealed by many thousands of experiments.

Organization and direction, the direct opposite of chance, imply purpose. So the fields of life offer purely electronic, instrumental evidence that man is no accident. On the contrary, he is an integral part of the Cosmos, embedded in its all-powerful fields, subject to its inflexible laws and a participant in the destiny and purpose of the Universe.

This book is an account of the adventure in science—of the long, step-by-step exploration—that wrested from Nature the answer to the question which so many in these times are asking so anxiously.

2

Electro-dynamic fields are invisible and intangible; and it is hard to visualize them. But a crude analogy may help to show what the fields of life—L-fields for short—do and why they are so important:

Most people who have taken high-school science will remember that if iron-filings are scattered on a card held over a magnet they will arrange themselves in the pattern of the 'lines of force' of the magnet's field. And if the filings are thrown away and fresh ones scattered on the card, the new filings will assume the same pattern as the old.

Something like this—though infinitely more complicated—happens in the human body. Its molecules and cells are constantly being torn apart and rebuilt with fresh material from the food we eat. But, thanks to the controlling L-field, the new molecules and cells are rebuilt as before and arrange themselves in the same pattern as the old ones.

Modern research with 'tagged' elements has revealed that the materials of our bodies and brains are renewed much more often than was previously realized. All the protein in the body, for example, is 'turned over' every six months and, in some organs such as the liver, the protein is renewed more frequently. When we meet a friend we have not seen for six months there is not one molecule in his face which was there when we last saw him. But, thanks to his controlling L-field, the new molecules have fallen into the old, familiar pattern and we can recognize his face.

Until modern instruments revealed the existence of the controlling L-fields, biologists were at a loss to explain how our bodies 'keep in shape' through ceaseless metabolism and changes of material. Now the mystery has been solved, the electro-dynamic field of the body serves as a matrix or mould, which preserves the 'shape' or arrangement of any material poured into it, however often the material may be changed.

When a cook looks at a jelly-mould she knows the shape of the jelly she will turn out of it. In much the same way, inspection with instruments of an L-field in its initial stage can reveal the future 'shape' or arrangement of the materials it will mould. When the L-field in a frog's egg, for instance, is examined electrically it is possible to show the future location of the frog's nervous system because the frog's L-field is the matrix which will determine the form which will develop from the egg. (See page 61.)

Inspection of L-fields is done with special voltmeters and electrodes—to be described shortly—which reveal different patterns or gradients of voltages in different parts of the L-field.

To return to the cook, when she uses a battered mould she expects to find some dents or bulges in the jelly. Similarly, a 'battered' L-field—that is, one with abnormal voltage-patterns —can give warning of something 'out of shape' in the body, sometimes in advance of actual symptoms.

For example, malignancy in the ovary has been revealed by L-field measurements before any clinical sign could be observed. Such measurements, therefore, could help doctors to detect cancer early, when there is a better chance of treating it successfully. (See page 54 and Dr. Langman's paper in Part II.)

Nature keeps an infinite variety of electro-dynamic 'jelly-moulds' on her shelves with which she shapes the countless different forms of life that exist on this planet. L-fields have been detected and measured not only in men and women but also in animals, trees, plants, seeds, eggs and even in one of the lowest forms of life, slime-moulds.

Of these L-fields, those of trees can tell something that others cannot because trees do not move about, live to a great age and can be hitched up to recording instruments for long periods of time. For many years a maple tree in New Haven and an elm in Old Lyme were continuously connected to recording voltmeters —something which, obviously, cannot be done with men and women.

These long records showed that the L-fields of trees vary not only with sunlight and darkness but also with the cycles of the moon, with magnetic storms and with sunspots. (See page 97 and Mr. Markson's paper in Part II.)

If such extra-terrestrial forces can influence the relatively-simple L-fields of trees we would expect them to have an even greater influence on the more complex L-fields of men and women; and there is evidence that they do.

These sturdy Connecticut trees, then, have helped to answer the question which philosophers have disputed for centuries and which many ask so anxiously today. For they have shown that life on this planet is not isolated from the Universe but a part of it—susceptible to those irresistible forces that exert their influence across the vast distances of space.

3

L-fields are detected and examined by measuring the difference in voltage between two points on—or close to—the surface of the living form. In men and women L-field voltages can be measured by placing one electrode on the forehead and the other on the chest or the hand. Alternatively, the index finger of each hand is dipped into bowls of saline solution connected to the voltmeter. In special cases voltage readings may be taken by applying the electrodes to some specific organ or part of the body.

In trees, the electrodes are in contact through salt bridges with the cambium layer, one about two feet above the other.

These voltage measurements have nothing to do with the alternating electrical currents which doctors find in the heart and the brain. They are pure voltage *potentials* which can yield only an infinitesimal amount of *direct* current. That is why L-fields could not be detected before the invention of the vacuum-tube voltmeter, which requires virtually no current for its operation. An ordinary voltmeter needs so much current to swing the needle that it would drain away the L-field potentials and make any reading useless if not impossible.

When Sir John Fleming, an Englishman, discovered that electrons flow from a heated wire in a vacuum and Lee DeForest, an American, found out how to use them with a grid, it is unlikely that either of them ever imagined that the vacuum tube which resulted from their discoveries would one day make possible a new approach to the mystery of life. And it was many years before the vacuum tube had been sufficiently perfected to make the vacuum-tube voltmeter a reliable instrument.

In the early days of his researches, some forty years ago, the author spent three years developing his own instruments. Today highly sensitive and reliable vacuum-tube voltmeters are available commercially and are to be found in most physics laboratories and electronic factories.

There is nothing mysterious, then, about the instruments required to measure L-field voltages. But these are harder to measure than those of a car or transistor-radio battery. Special electrodes must be used and the methods outlined in Chapter 2 must be followed rigidly and explicitly for successful results. But it will be no more difficult to train doctors and their assistants to read and interpret L-field voltages than it was to train them to use electro-cardiographs or electro-encephalographs.

Extensive medical use of L-field readings, however, may not be seen for some time. For it took over thirty years before electrocardiograph techniques were perfected to the point where they were useful in doctors' offices.

4

In the case of L-fields there is no technical reason why their use by doctors should take so long. Modern instruments are reliable; and any intelligent man or woman can learn the techniques of taking and interpreting L-field readings in a short period of intensive instruction. It is to be hoped that many will do so because L-fields can be helpful to doctors, psychiatrists and others in various ways.

Immediate and practical results, in fact, can stem from this adventure in science—quite apart from the assurance that human life has purpose and that man is not isolated from the Universe —which have made the adventure even more worthwhile.

As mentioned earlier, abnormalities in L-field voltages can give advance warning of future symptoms before these are evident. This does not apply only to the early detection of cancer. As more research is done and L-fields are better understood, it is probable that they will be used to give early warning of a variety of physical problems in time to tackle these effectively. And they have already been used to forecast certain psychological and psychiatric troubles. (See page 18 and Dr. Ravitz' paper in Part II.)

Among the physical events which can be predicted by measuring the voltage-gradients is the precise moment of ovulation in a woman. This is possible because ovulation is preceded by a steady and substantial rise in voltage, which falls rapidly to normal after the egg has been released.

Such measurements have revealed that some women may ovulate over the entire menstrual period, that ovulation may occur without mestruation and menses without ovulation. The potential importance of this knowledge to gynaecology, family-planning and birth-control is obvious; and it helps to explain why the 'rhythm method' of birth-control is inadequate.

A patient of the author's, a married woman, made good use of her L-field. For years she and her husband had longed in vain to have children. So, over a period of weeks, she made regular visits to the author's office and herself measured the voltages in her own L-field by dipping her fingers into bowls of solution connected to a voltmeter. When, one day, she saw her voltages rising rapidly, she knew that ovulation was imminent and went to her husband. A longed-for child was the result.

Wounds—even a small cut on the finger—will change the voltages in the L-field and, as the wound heals, these will return to normal. This offers surgeons a simple, reliable way to measure

16

the rate of healing, which will be specially useful with internal wounds from operations. (See page 82.)

L-field measurements are not only useful in diagnosing local conditions; they can also be used to assess the general state of the body as a whole. For these pure voltage-differences—independent of any current flow or changes in skin-resistance—reveal the state of the whole human force-field. Such conditions, then, as ovulation or malignancy can be detected by measuring changes in the L-field of the body *at a distance from the affected organs.* And, as the force-field extends beyond the surface of the skin, it is sometimes possible to measure field-voltages with the electrodes a short distance from the surface of the skin—*not* in contact with it. *This shows that it is a true field that is measured and not some surface potential.*

This, too, is additional evidence that L-fields have the same qualities as the simpler fields of physics because they can produce an effect across a space or gap, without any visible intervening means.

Since L-fields reveal the state of the body as a whole they can be used to assess the general effects of drugs, sleep or hypnosis. Dr. Leonard J. Ravitz, Jr., has not only measured the depth of hypnosis with a voltmeter but has also found that strong emotions recalled during hypnosis can cause a voltage-rise of as much as from 15 to 20 millivolts. (See page 87 and Dr. Ravitz' paper in Part II.)

This suggests the fascinating possibility that psychiatrists of the future will be able to measure the intensity of grief, anger or love electrically—and as easily as we measure temperature or noise-levels today. 'Heartbreak', hate, or love, in other words, may one day be measurable in millivolts.

Good doctors have always known how important it is to consider the patient as a whole—to take into account his mental or emotional state as well as his physical symptoms—because many human ills have a 'psychosomatic' cause. Business worries or an unhappy marriage are often the real cause of, say, headaches or ulcers. Since L-field voltages reveal both physical and mental conditions they can offer doctors a new insight into the state of both body and mind.

When the effects on the human L-field of extraterrestrial forces are established and understood, this knowledge will be important in the study not only of human health and behaviour but also of medical problems which may arise in long space explorations. The fields of space may have unforseen effects on the L-fields of astronauts if they are exposed to them for long periods.

5

This adventure in science promises still further 'dividends' in the form of a better understanding of the human mind.

Dr. Ravitz has discovered that the voltages of the L-fields of healthy people are not constant but vary in steady rhythms over periods of weeks—whatever the cause may be. From plotting over 30,000 measurements on 430 human subjects he has found that these rhythms show how the subjects feel. When they feel 'on top of the world' their voltages are high; when they feel 'below par' their voltages are low.

For healthy, normal people these voltage rhythms can be plotted as steady regular curves which alter little over long periods. From these curves, then, it is *possible to predict in advance* when the individual will be at his best and when he will be feeling 'below par'.

This knowledge could be of vital importance to those engaged in hazardous duties, especially in the Armed Forces. If commanding officers had advance knowledge of the 'low' periods of, say, combat pilots, they could try to avoid sending them on dangerous missions at times when their alertness and efficiency would be reduced. If operational necessity made that impossible, at least this knowledge might warn the men to use special vigilance and care.

Intelligently used, warnings offered by the state of the L-fields could save valuable lives and equipment not only in the Armed Forces but also in dangerous industrial occupations.

With emotionally-unstable people the voltage variations cannot be plotted as steady regular curves. They display an erratic pattern which, in many cases, can be detected within a few days. By purely objective, electronic means, therefore, it will be possible for the Armed Forces quickly to detect and weed out emotionally-unstable personnel before time and money are spent on training them for duties for which they are not fitted.

Similarly, industry will be able not only to avoid hiring personnel who might 'crack' under responsibility but also to find those best qualified to assume greater responsibilities.

Since L-field voltages reflect mental and emotional states they can also be useful in the handling of mental patients because they offer doctors an objective measurement of progress. Thus they can help to prevent the release of patients who might be a danger to the public; they can also help doctors to decide when it is safe to release others—with a great saving of hospital space and taxpayers' money.

Voltage measurements used in this kind of psychological testing are completely impersonal and reproducible. There is no need to question the patient; the technician who takes the readings need not open his mouth.

In the medical laboratories of the future, it is probable that trained technicians will take the voltage-readings and then submit these to a doctor qualified to interpret them, in much the same way as technicians take X-ray photographs and submit them to a radiologist. 'Voltage-interpreters', however, need not be as specialized as radiologists; and many doctors in the future will be their own interpreters.

6

Since L-fields have been found in all living forms examined so far, their potential usefulness is not limited to medical diagnosis.

In measuring the L-fields of plants, for instance, it has been found that the change of a single gene in the parent stock produces profound changes in the voltage-pattern. This phenomenon could be of great importance in the study of genetics in plants and in animals. (See page 70.)

By measuring the L-fields of seeds it is possible to predict how strong and healthy the future plants will be. To have advance knowledge of the future vitality of living forms could be useful in many fields. (See page 71.)

Since the fields of life are dominant and control the growth and development of all living forms, medical science may one day find ways directly to treat the health of the patient electrically before the onset of physical symptoms.

Agricultural scientists of the future may, perhaps, find ways to stimulate the growth of crops electrically and to eliminate defects in their L-fields which render them prone to pests or diseases. It has long been known not only that sunlight—a form of electro-magnetic radiation—is essential to the growth of most plant life but also that different species require different 'dosages' of sunlight. It is known, too, that certain frequencies or colours of light are beneficial in specific cases. It may one day be discovered, then, that other and invisible electro-magnetic frequencies have beneficial effects on the L-fields of plants.

Since animals and plants possess—and are controlled by—their characteristic L-fields, like man they are an integral part of the Universe and subject to its laws. So the human race and the animal and vegetable kingdoms are component parts of the same whole. You and I, our pets, our trees and our plants are all subject to the same universal laws.

This is borne out by the mutual interdependence of species. Plants depend for their existence on sunlight—an extraterrestrial force; plants nourish man and animals; animals feed on each other. So when we remember that we should starve without sunlight from some ninety-three million miles away, it is not hard to accept that we are subject to the other great forces of space.

7

It has taken only a few pages to summarize some of the results of this adventure in science for the benefit of the impatient reader. But the adventure itself occupied many years because Nature does not share human impatience and is in no hurry to yield her secrets. Those, therefore, who expect instant answers from Nature are likely to be disappointed.

Nature, too, does not effect instant improvements; she may

take an aeon to evolve something better. And as we are all a part of Nature and subject to her laws, those who expect an immediate improvement of human nature or an instant answer to some human problem are likely to suffer from acute frustration.

However impatient for results they may be, scientists realize that they cannot impose their will or their desires on Nature; they must follow her methods and meet her conditions. This may explain why, in this age, science is usually more successful in solving its problems than politics.

Perhaps, then, a description of this particular adventure in science may serve a dual purpose: while it will give the evidence that man is linked to the Universe and subject to its laws it will also illustrate the scientific method by which the laws and secrets of Nature may be discovered.

This has more than an academic interest at the present time when respect for man-made laws is decreasing and many feel that laws are made to be disobeyed. Natural laws, however, cannot be disobeyed; we cannot flout, for example, the law of gravity. So the more we can find out about Nature's laws—and also about how science discovers them—the easier it will be for us to accept the need for laws and to realize that man-made laws reflect—however imperfectly—the essential principles of a Universe of law and order.

Unfortunately, there is much confusion about the meaning of the word 'science'. The dictionary defines it as 'organized knowledge'. But, beginning probably with Galileo, the experimental method—with its enormous development since that time—has revealed that it is not enough to describe and classify the Universe in general and the earth in particular. It is also necessary to attempt to find the meaning of all the facts that have been accumulated.

This involves trying to understand the relation between the component parts of the Universe—an understanding that must always be developing and changing as the experimental method uncovers more facts. All that can be done is to interpret the facts as best we can, always bearing in mind that our knowledge is still tragically incomplete.

Science, therefore, means not only the collection of facts and the classification and description of the physical components of the Universe but also a consideration of the laws or forces which govern the relation between these components.

This, of course, requires a primitive assumption: that the Universe is a place of law and order which—it is to be hoped—can be understood by the mind of man.

There are many who maintain that the Universe is chaos, that the only law and order in it are those which are imposed by the mind of man—a far more primitive assumption. For, however great our respect for the powers of the human mind, it is difficult to see how man can impose the arrangements and movements of the stars in their courses or, as far as we on this earth are concerned, the nature of the forces which define a living system.

It should be reasonably clear to any thinking person that nothing in the Universe could exist for a fraction of a millisecond if there were not forces, laws and organization which determine the relationship between the component parts of the Universe, all of which—from a galaxy to the particles of an atom—are in constant motion. No living organism could exist if the process of living were not regulated by meticulous and powerful forces, about which it is obviously desirable to find out as much as we can.

Our primitive assumption, then, that the Universe is a place of law and order is justified by both observation and common sense. The many successes of the experimental method also justify the hope that we can learn more and more about the laws of the Universe.

This has enormous implications for man because it follows that man is not only *in* the Universe but also *of* the Universe, subject to laws in the living world similar to those which can be recognized and understood in the material Universe.

At once we are faced with a curious anomaly. Many people object to the idea of law and order in the Universe on the ground that it is authoritarian and impinges on man's free will to develop his own ways of doing things on his own responsibility. Yet these same people would not dream of defying the law of gravity, which, so far as we know, is a universal property of the Universe, and, in fact, are fully prepared to adjust to it—especially when walking on an icy sidewalk.

Not only do we have to pay attention to the law of gravity but also to learn as much about it as possible so that it can be put to the service of man, whether in emptying a bathtub or for getting astronauts safely back from space. This is true not only of the law of gravity but also of all other natural laws that can be discovered.

8

All this raises an important problem. Though many concede that the Universe may be dominated by physical laws, they maintain that man is not a part of this physical Universe but is a separate, spiritual being, subject to spiritual law. This at once denies the unity of the Universe, for it means that there are two sets of laws, the laws of the material Universe and the laws of the spiritual component of the Universe.

Physical laws, determined by experiment, can be validated and can be found to be true not only in New York but also in Timbuktu. Spiritual laws, on the other hand, which are inventions of the mind of man, have one set of meanings in the Western hemisphere and a quite different one in the East.

This concept of two kinds of law make any generally-accepted understanding of the nature of man and his part in the Universe well-nigh impossible.

Spiritual laws, to be sure, are believed to have been validated in the experience of man and, within certain limits, this is probably true. But laws which have different meanings in different parts of the world—and, sometimes, different meanings to different people in the same part of the world—are not compatible with physical laws which are universally verifiable and accepted.

This is the cause of the conflict between science and religion. It is the basic argument of religion that the intuitive, creative imagination of man can set up laws which transcend physical law and which describe aspects of nature which, otherwise, cannot be validated. It is the argument—or, perhaps, the hope—of science that all aspects of Nature are open to examination by the experimental method. It is true that, for centuries, this method has been limited to certain aspects of Nature. But it has been so successful that science sees no reason why, eventually, it should not be extended to all aspects.

Curiously enough, the scientific method is not confined to science but is something by which most of us live all the time. First of all we find out all we can about a problem as a basis for its solution; and, in the process somewhere along the line, we see some unsuspected relationships between the facts we have uncovered. Then we have a hunch, a guess, a dream or, to use a technical term, a hypothesis, though nobody knows how these creative ideas arise.

This hunch or hypothesis suggests some logical deductions, which we can check in various ways to see if they offer a solution to our problem.

In a physics laboratory it is not too hard to check a hypothesis by rigidly controlled experiments and, if these support it, it is generally assumed that it is correct. But when it comes to human problems or the problems of other living organisms it is usually much more difficult to check an hypothesis.

In any event we should not make the mistake of assuming that because experiments support the hypothesis the latter is the *only* one those experiments could support. This makes it difficult to achieve any final, conclusive answer, which is probably just as well because if it were easy to get unequivocal, demonstrated answers to everything we would lose a lot of the fun of living.

This process—fact-finding, hypothesis, deduction and experiment—is one in which most of us engage all the time. For example, on the basis of our knowledge of the performance of the horses running at Louisville, we make the logical deduction that Northern Dancer will win the stakes and place our bet that this will happen. If the horse wins we assume that our guess, hunch or hypothesis was valid. If he loses, we have to accept that it was not.

This is true not only of horse-races and ball-games but also of almost every other aspect of the activity of the mind of man. An artist sees in the beauty of the world around him something which he thinks is important and at once begins to depict it. An author has an idea which he expresses in writing. The musician conceives a piece of music and composes it. We all do the same thing in our various forms of activity. But it is often difficult to know if our original idea was a good one.

If the picture is purchased, if the book becomes a best-seller and if the music is played all over the country, the creators of these things can assume—within limits—that their original flight of imagination was worthwhile. But such confirmation is not always available and, if it is not, that does not necessarily prove that the flight of imagination was worthless because many important ideas have lain dormant or unrecognized for many years.

There is nothing mysterious, then, about the way in which scientists attempt to discover natural laws. We all use the same method but scientists enjoy an advantage over non-scientists: it is usually easier for them to check their hunches by experiments.

For both scientists and non-scientists, problem-solving must always be a developing, growing process, subject to change as knowledge and understanding increase. To say, therefore, that something has been proven is often questionable, except in a few cases, such as the law of gravity, which we can say have been proven beyond question. To increase the number of things which can be regarded as proven is, of course, the ultimate desire of all students of the Universe, but that desire is not often achieved.

To some this may seem a pessimistic approach, depriving man of his essential dignity. This is, of course, far from the truth because the complexity of the Universe and its component parts is so great that the mind of any individual can only analyse a few of the complexities and interpret them in the light of such information as may be available. A modest approach to an understanding of the Universe does not impair human dignity—it enhances it. Moreover, it is the only approach likely to succeed because Nature seems reluctant to reveal her secrets to the intellectually arrogant.

These, then, are the methods and the approach which have been adopted in the present adventure in science.

CHAPTER TWO
The Course and the Compass

1

In the previous chapter we outlined some of the results of this adventure in science. But it should be emphasized that when we set out we knew what we hoped to find but had no certainty of finding it.

For science is a trip across uncharted seas to a goal which lies beyond the horizon. We do not know the *ultimate* goal. All we can hope for is that there is some goal which we ourselves can reach or, if we cannot find it, that we can get near enough to it to learn some more about it and to pave the way for others to follow us.

Though he already knows some of the things we found, the reader may be interested to know how we found them, as an illustration of the scientific method, just as many are interested to read an account of some expedition, of which they already know the result.

However uncertain the ultimate goal, we could not, of course, set sail at random. Like all explorers we had to have some idea of what we were looking for, even though we realized that we might not find it or might come upon something we never thought of, like an early explorer who thought he was on the way to China and found what today is Montreal.

As explained in the last chapter we had to assemble all the facts we could, to seek some connection between them and then to formulate a hunch or hypothesis which we hoped to prove by our voyage of discovery.

Before we could set out, however, we had to look for the best navigational instruments we could find to keep us on our projected course.

2

Since the time of Galvani there have been innumerable studies of living organisms, all of which make it abundantly clear that all living organisms possess electrical properties. In our own day and generation, brain waves, heart waves, concomitants of nervous impulses, of muscle contraction and of glandular activity have filled the literature with a great deal of exceedingly important information. The meaning of all these phenomena has been worked out almost entirely on an empirical basis. Relations of electrical phenomena with many biological functions in health and in disease have been observed.

There has been no general underlying theory, however, of the nature and the meaning of the recorded electrical changes, except in so far as they can be explained by their consequences. The reason for this is fairly obvious: Modern emphasis on entities, on fluid forms, atomicity and discontinuity, has dominated biological thought.

Galileo had no sooner developed his physical and mechanical theory of the inorganic universe, than Harvey proceeded to apply physical and mechanical conceptions to living creatures in the discovery of the circulation of the blood. Levoisier revealed the chemical character of respiration in metabolism in living things at the same time that he placed chemistry upon a secure foundation with the discovery of the principle of the conservation of mass. Gradually, with Liebig and a vast army of physiological chemists, the chemical nature of living creatures became more and more evident.

It is to be noted that this is a distinctly modern emphasis. Chemistry rests upon a discontinuous, atomic conception of nature. Atomism, in its traditional interpretation, involved an emphasis on entities, rather than upon structure, and on constituent elements, rather than on the whole. This attitude of mind has gone all through biology even where no thought has been given to the chemical nature of the processes or factors considered. Practically a century ago, Schleiden and Schwann discovered the cellular nature of plants and animals. Here, supposedly, was the ultimate biological atom. More recently, emphasis has shifted from the cell to the gene, and from that to the highly complex protein molecule capable of replication. But even so, the emphasis is still on entities. *—physical*

It is to be noted that this entire development involved the carrying over into biology of a philosophical standpoint which was discovered and clearly formulated first in physics and chemistry. There can be no doubt of its success or its validity. There is nothing to date to indicate that biologists should hesitate to follow the lead which the mature and exact science of physics gives them. But, if they are faithfully to follow this lead, it is clear that a slight change of emphasis should come into biological theory. For in physics the former emphasis on entities rather than on organization, upon discontinuity, rather than upon continuity, upon local systems, rather than upon their status in the total field of nature as a whole, has been found to need a radical and thoroughgoing supplementation.

The word *supplementation* is to be emphasized, for modern standpoints have not rejected the former emphasis; it is merely being amended. The amendment is so thoroughgoing, however, as to amount to the placing of the Greek upon an equal footing with the modern standpoint. Moreover, the concepts modified are so primary, so important and so general and universal in their application that every branch of human activity—and even the very meaning and significance of any fact we observe or of any experiment we perform—are affected. The elemental and essential fact as it appears in physics can be stated very briefly.

Atomic physics has had to be supplemented with field physics. The point to be noted is that the particle both conditions and is conditioned by its field. Stated in more general terms, this means that continuity, as well as discontinuity, is ultimate, that Nature is both one and many. In short, any local system in part, constitutes—and, in part, is constituted in its behaviour by— Nature as a whole and the physical field in which it is embedded.

This rediscovery of the continuous field—or the one, as causal factor conditioning the behaviour of the constituent particles or the many—is a return to the Greek standpoint. But the particles

28

also determine the character of the field. This is the modern viewpoint. The reciprocal causal relationship between field and particle amounts to the union of both viewpoints. This is the fact that anyone with an eye to first principles can see standing out amid all the complexities of the confusions of current discoveries in physics.*

But this mere designation of the fact is not enough. We do not possess science until our findings are formulated in terms of clear, consistent principles. The modern conception of Nature as a discontinuous collection of moving particles makes all order in Nature a temporary effect, renders Nature as a whole a mere aggregate and provides no meaning for the continuity as a primary factor or for the field as a causal factor. The Greek conception as formulated in mathematics and astronomy by Plato and Eudoxius, or in biology by Aristotle, does justice to continuity, unity and organization—and also to the field character of natural phenomena—but at the cost of interpreting Nature as a single substance or system.

It is clear, therefore, that before the doctrine of reciprocal interaction between particle and field can be made significant a new theory of the first principles of science must be developed. Moreover, this new theory must combine the Greek and modern conceptions of science which previously were supposed to be incompatible. It is essential to realize the necessity of this theoretical formulation before going further because, otherwise, the electro-dynamic theory of life will appear merely as a new name for traditional conceptions and its essential novelty and significance will be lost.

The theory, however, means more than this. The microscopic physico-chemical constituents do determine in part the character of the field. No one cognizant of modern physics and physiological chemistry can deny this, but this relationship between field and particle is not, as traditional modern scientific theory has assumed, an asymmetrical or one-way relation. The field both determines and is determined.

To understand that the field determines the behaviour of any local process or constituent, it is necessary fundamentally to

*Cf. F. S. C. Northrop, 'Science and first Principles'.

modify modern science by revising our theory of first principles in order to justify the unity of Nature as a causal factor. Without this revision of our most elemental concept of Nature, as conceived by science, all field theories, whether in physiology or physics, are mere verbiage.

Einstein has shown that the apparently constant macroscopic structure of space is the approximately constant microscopic structure of matter itself. The field is not independent of matter, but an appropriate determinant of the behaviour of matter. Thus, Einstein replaces Newton's three laws of motion with a single law, that a body moves in a path in the space time of the observer's frame of reference. But the general theory of relativity also prescribes that the distribution of matter determines the character of the field. Thus the particle both conditions and is conditioned by the metrical field.

We can see the significance of this for biology if we reconsider its most fundamental and perplexing problem, the problem of organization. It is a commonplace that living creatures, not withstanding the modification in types in evolution, maintain a certain constancy in structure through continuous changes of material. The traditional modern doctrine, that the chemical elements determine the structure and organization of the organism, fails to explain why a certain structural constancy persists despite continuous metabolism and chemical flux. This obvious inadequacy led to the introduction of non-physical factors, such as Driesch's entelechy, Spehmann's organizer, Child's physiological gradients, Weiss's biological field, all of which have certain validity as descriptive terms.

It now appears, however, that the difficulty is not in the failure of any possible theory, but in the inadequacy of traditional theory. For—in spite of the mass of accumulated data concerning the development of the organism, in general, and of the nervous system, in particular—no thoroughly satisfactory explanation has been given of the regulation of the control of growth. Description of successive steps of development in a wide variety of forms reveals little of the relationships which exist between the steps or the factors which regulate the passage from one to another. The very wealth of the accumulated facts tends to obscure the underlying regulation and to defy analysis.

It was this difficulty that led Driesch to postulate a vital force of entelechy. This brilliant hypothesis has never received its just due. The whole theory is a very adequate description of an extraordinary constant control and regulation of growth. Its weakness lay in its assumption of an extra-biological agent incapable of scientific description. The field theories of Spehmann, Weiss, and Gurwitsch are also valuable attempts at explanation but, like the entelechies of Driesch, scientific analysis is well-nigh impossible.

It is well known to every biologist that each biological system seems to possess a dynamic wholeness, the maintenance of whose integrity is a necessity of continued existence. Virtually all the theoretical analyses stress this quality, but no adequate definition of its dynamic agent or adequate explanation of its working has been offered. A considerable body of information is available concerning the physical and chemical structure of protoplasm, but we know little of the way in which the elements are organized into a dynamic whole.

The cytoplasm of a living cell is not a formless conglomeration of chemical substances, but is an integrated and co-ordinated system. It is impossible to conceive a cytoplasm as a haphazard arrangement of molecules. A definite pattern of relationships must exist. We possess a modicum of knowledge of these relationships at any one moment, but we have no adequate theory of the mechanism which maintains that pattern throughout the rapidly changing flux in living systems. The difficulties suggested above are no less apparent in the analysis of the development of the nervous system. Its successive steps have been described by innumerable workers. We lack any rational explanation of the appearance of local regions of growth and differentiation and of the final establishment of nuclear masses in fibre tract pathways.

3

With the advent in physics of the field theory of the relationship between particulate matter, the resolution of the biological theory becomes clear. We believed that the electro-dynamic theory would satisfy this condition and if it could be demonstrated, would solve many problems of biology.

The theory is the result of many years of experimental investigation of the mechanisms involved in the nervous system.* In these studies it has been shown[†] that an extremely important factor in the organization of the nervous system is the rise and fall of differential growth rates within the wall of the neural tube. Moreover, experimental work confirms the belief that the direction of growth and the end station of differentiating nerve fibres is related to these primary centres of rapid proliferation. Since they seem to be potent factors in imparting the fibre pattern of the nervous system, it is necessary to examine the agents which could act to determine the locus areas and to regulate the division rates within them. If these could be established it would be possible to formulate an hypothesis as to the origin of pattern in the nervous system. Conceivably, this might provide a clue to the origin of the pattern in developing organisms and in other living systems.

An increasing body of evidence[‡] indicates that bioelectrical phenomena underlie growth as well as many other biological processes. Numerous bioelectrical studies compel us to believe that polar and potential differences exist in living systems. *If this is true, it follows by definition that electro-dynamic fields are also present.*

Their existence in the physical world is generally accepted. Moreover, the interrelationship of particulate matter is, to a considerable degree, a function of such fields. Thus the individual

---

* See papers by Burr, H. S., 1916a and b, 1920, 1924, 1926, 1930, 1932. Details in Appendix.

† Burr, H. S., 1932. Details in Appendix.

‡ Gurwich, 1926; Ingvar, 1920; Lund, 1922.

characteristics of atomic matter are a result of the interdependence of fields and particles. Pattern in physics, then, is determined
by the interplay of electro-dynamic fields and the particular
matter therein contained.

It is reasonable to extend this hypothesis into the realms of
biology. Potential gradients and polar differences exist in living
systems. Since this is so, then electro-dynamic fields are also
present.

*The following theory may then be formulated. The pattern or
organization of any biological system is established by a complex
electro-dynamic field which is in part determined by its atomic
physio-chemical components and which in part determines the
behaviour and orientation of those components. This field is
electrical in the physical sense and by its properties relates the
entities of the biological system in a characteristic pattern and
is itself, in part, a result of the existence of those entities. It determines and is determined by the components.*

More than establishing pattern, it must maintain pattern in
the midst of a physio-chemical flux. Therefore, it must regulate
and control living things. It must be the mechanism, the outcome
of whose activity is wholeness, organization, and continuity.
The electro-dynamic field, then, is comparable to the entelechy of
Driesch, the embryonic field of Spehmann, and the biological
field of Weiss.

The Electro-Dynamic Theory of Life stated above was developed with the collaboration of Dr. F. S. C. Northrop, of Yale,
and was first put forward in a joint paper in 1935.*

This theory yields a number of interesting implications for
embryology, only one of which can be considered here: An intriguing problem in development of a tail is the establishment
of a longitudinal axis. This is a very real structure alignment,
although at early stages of development the cells which are related to it are not specialized. For experimental rearrangment of
these cellular units does not change the axis, although they themselves have their ultimate fate altered. Caudal cells may become
cephalic cells, right cells may become left cells with little serious

* Burr, H. S. and Northrop, F. S. C., *Quarterly Review of Biology*
10: 322-333, 1935.

interference with the processes of growth. Yet in some way, the constituent cells of the growing system have their state determined and their behaviour and orientation controlled.

To Driesch we owe the brilliant observation that the fate of any group of cells in an embryo is not only genetically conditioned, but is also the result of the position of that group of cells in the biological whole. The mechanism by which position could determine cellular potencies was explained by Driesch through an assumption of an extra biological guiding principle, an entelechy. It is at this point that the electro-dynamic field theory proposed above provides a significant explanation of the well-recognized facts. In the physical world, the nature of an atom is dependent upon the number of entities which comprise it and the field in which they lie, the position of the electron orbits being of fundamental importance. So, in a very much more complex scale in the biological system, the fate of any group of cells is determined in part by the positions those cells occupy in the electro-dynamic field in the embryo. It is clear, that if the above is granted, three factors are present in the normal development of an organism. The cells must possess a certain genetic constitution, certain cellular environment, and certain positions in the electro-dynamic field.

4

The theoretical considerations here presented led us to the conclusion, reached by nearly all investigators, that pattern or organization is a fundamental characteristic of biological systems or of physical systems, or of the Universe. The electro-dynamic theory provided a working hypothesis for a direct attack upon this problem and we felt that it should be possible to determine by objective experiment whether or not such fields exist; in other words, that this theory could be put to experimental test. If accepted, it could open up a wide field of study based on electrometric methods. It could also make it possible to place the investigation of the organization of living systems on the same objective and physical basis as the analysis of their chemical constituents.

It appeared, therefore, that an hypothesis of this type was necessary to bring biological theory into line with physical theory. Moreover, biological considerations themselves affirmed a similar necessity and provided sufficient data to warrant putting to Nature, by experimental and electric methods, the questions which this theory raises.

These questions fall naturally into three categories. In the first of these are questions as to the presence of potential and polar differences in living systems. In the second, are the questions dealing with the measurements of electro-dynamic fields which accompany the potential differences. In the third category are questions concerning the interrelationship between electric fields of the environment and the fields of the developing mechanism.

If the theory could be established, we felt it would be possible to apply the mathematical methods developed for field physics to biological material. This would place the study of biological organization on a mathematical as well as on an experimental basis.

The general statement of the field theory here presented required that four questions be put to Nature: The first, Are there potential and polar differences in living systems everywhere? The second, Do these potential differences exist in an organized fashion, or are they chaotic and indeterminate? The third, Are the electrical measurements made in the laboratory a valid measure of an electro-dynamic field? The fourth, If the field exists, does it control or determine the living process or is it a consequence—or a mere accompaniment—of that process?

5

We now knew what we were looking for, but before we could set sail, we had to obtain a suitable 'compass' with which to navigate these unknown seas. But, some thirty-five years ago when this adventure was projected, no suitable 'compass' existed.

Up to that time, all electrical measurements of living systems

35

had been made with instruments which were operated by the electrical output of the system. Needless to say, this drained the current from the system, which was badly disturbed by the measuring.

The brilliant exception was Lund who, in his early experiments used an electrometer to study living organisms. But everyone who has worked with these instruments knows that they are difficult to set up and to keep in good operating condition for sufficiently-long periods to permit careful study of the living organism.

Lund made another great advance by using zinc sulphate electrodes in tap water or cell sap to make contact with the protoplasm itself. This technique avoided the unpredictable and unreliable measurements made by others with metal electrodes in contact with the protoplasm. Such contact always gives rise to artificial potentials not related to the system being measured: and the resulting measurements are unreliable.

One has only to read Lund's papers to realize what an incredibly rigorous technique was demanded by his studies. He not only used a Compton electrometer, which draws no current from the system measured, but also reasonably-reversible electrodes. And many of his earlier experiments were carried out under stable environmental conditions with controlled stimuli of the protoplasm. It seemed desirable to find an instrument easier to use and more reliable over long periods.

At the outset, it seemed probable that if potential differences could be measured in living systems they would be very small. An alternative to the electrometer, therefore, had to be devised which would draw little or no current from the system being measured. In other words, the instrument must not disturb the system. For it seemed likely that the great confusion in biometric measurements of the past had been caused by the lack of any such instrument in biological laboratories.

A series of rather extensive specifications was set up. First, the device must consist of an amplifier with a very high input impedance so that resistance changes in the system itself would have little effect upon the measurement. Second, the instrument, or amplifier, must be of sufficient sensitivity to record minor changes in the electrical voltage gradients. Third, the device must necessarily be stable so that random fluctuations would be reduced to a minimum.

Another specification was that the amplifier and the system being measured should not require external shielding. This meant a high rejection-rate at the input to the amplifier. Finally, obviously if an instrument of this kind was to be used effectively in biological studies, it should be portable and reliable and not too expensive. This latter condition was met by using standard radio parts, necessarily the best radio parts which could be found.

The original instrument, built in the 1930s, following the design of Dr. Cecil Lane of the Physics Department of Yale University, used the then readily-available 112-A vacuum tube. In those days, such tubes were excellent vacuum tubes but they were in the process of development and it was difficult, therefore, to get two tubes that were reasonably balanced. A mathematical theory had been developed by Wynn-Williams for the theoretical balancing of somewhat dissimilar vacuum tubes. The tubes used were those having a large transconductance and were of the non-heater type, with relatively low temperature filament and a low plate impedance. This latter really defines the amplifier not as an amplifier, but as an impedance changer, converting the 10 million ohm input impedance to the relatively low ten thousand ohm output impedance. The actual amplification factor of the circuit was approximately one.

The tubes were so connected as to form two arms of a Wheatstone network; the other two arms are ordinary ohm resistance. Tube number one received the potential to be measured. Number two acted as a dummy, the function of which was to balance out the steady plate current of the input tube so that—with no potential difference impressed on the first tube—no current flowed through the galvanometer in the plate circuit of the output tube.

Upon impressing a potential difference upon the first tube, the effective resistance of this arm of the network is changed proportionally and a deflection of the galvanometer results. While it is admitted that this analysis is little more than a rough approximation, it has proved to be sufficient for the purposes herein described. It should be noted that a high transconductance is a necessary requirement.

A very important contribution to the theory of these devices was made by Wynn-Williams in the above-mentioned paper, when it was shown that it is possible to compensate automatically for the effect of filament battery variation. By operating the two tubes at slightly different filament voltages, a condition can be reached whereby a small fluctuation in the filament battery produced no variations in the current to the galvanometer. This is important since any strong battery shows slight variations in voltage, which in turn would lead to unsteadiness in the instrument zero.

The circuit described is of considerable value to the physicist for certain work, but its usefulness to the biologist is minimal. The principal reason for this lies in the fact that in all commercial vacuum tubes a current flows in any external circuit connecting the grid and the filament. This so-called grid current is independent, within considerable limits, of the resistance in the external circuit and, hence, will cause potential differences across resistors in the grid circuit in proportion to the value of the resistors. It is easy to see that if the specimen is connected across the input terminals, a fictitious potential difference will register on the galvanometer which may, in point of fact, be many times larger than the true potential difference. This, of course, would invalidate completely any results so obtained.

In order to convert the Wynn-Williams bridge into a practical biological instrument, it was obvious that the spurious grid current should be eliminated. The method employed to balance the grid current used the well-known principle of floating grid. It is known that if the grid of a vacuum tube otherwise operating normally is isolated from electric contact within the other element in the tube, the grid current will acquire a certain potential, a floating grid potential. If the grid is now biased by means of a battery to precisely this potential, it is found that the grid current is eliminated. In order to achieve this practically a variable grid bias on the input tube was employed in conjunction with the input switch. The value of the grid leak employed in the original instrument was chosen to be 10 megohms. The actual dynamic

38

input impedance of the 112-A at floating grid is probably several times higher than this figure, but 10 megohms has proved itself to be a good value in practice.

In the more than thirty years that these high input impedance amplifiers have been used, improvements have been made chiefly in the type of vacuum tube used. The basic circuit has not been altered, except that it has been possible to eliminate the Wynn-Williams balance because modern tubes are constructed with such rigorous controls that it is not difficult to get two tubes that are reasonably well balanced. It is interesting that over the last thirty years more and more amplifiers have been built with high input impedances, many of which are well above the 10 megohms used in this original and subsequent circuits. As a consequence, the reliability of the measurement has been enhanced very considerably.*

Once we had a reliable instrument to measure the very minute electrical voltages in living systems, the problem of connecting the instrument to the system became a matter of prime importance. For it was clear that in order to evaluate the potential gradients of a living system, an electrical circuit must be established in which only potentials arising in the system could affect the measuring instrument.

It is impossible to measure bioelectric potentials with any electrode in direct contact with living tissue, because an electrode, if reversible, has a potential conditioned by the connection of a particular ion or, if not reversible, has a potential of an unknown or uncertain magnitude. Electric contact can be made with a salt solution, however, if the salt be physiologically balanced with the ionic concentration of the system being measured, thus reducing to a minimum any potentials arising from a dissimilarity of fluids at the point of contact, or, if the salt solution be a normal environment, the contact potentials are, indeed, a part of the total bioelectric potential.

---

* Today sensitive and stable vacuum tube voltmeters are commercially available. A suitable American instrument for measuring L-fields is the Hewlett Packard DC Vacuum Tube Voltmeter Model 412A. See illustration. No doubt there are excellent European equivalents.

Of the known electrodes reversible to the ionic constituents of Ringer's solution, for example, only those reversible to the chlorine ion have been developed to the perfection demanded by this technique. For the range of chloride ion concentration found in solutions that are in physiological equilibrium, the silver chloride electrode is much more reproducible than the earlier much-used zinc electrode and can be used in the same solution that makes electrical contact with the living system, thereby avoiding liquid junction potentials. Silver chloride electrodes have been used by physical chemists in many exact electromotive force determinations and have been found to be stable and reproducible to within ten microvolts or better, when directly compared in the same solution.

The original electrodes were designated as Type Two by Harned and consisted of silver obtained by heating silver oxide, supported on a platinum wire, and silver chloride formed by subsequent electrolysis in a hydrochloric acid solution. These were complicated to make, cumbersome and difficult to apply practically in the field. Moreover, the original requirement that we should be able to measure voltage gradients down to a sensitivity of roughly ten microvolts, proved to be unimportant. In the beginning, however—since it was not clear from the literature just what magnitudes of the standing potential in living systems might be expected—it was necessary to aim at maximum sensitivity. Subsequently, however, many hundreds of thousands of determinations have made it abundantly clear that in most living systems, except perhaps the very small unicellular systems, the voltages developed are of the order of millivolts.

The current technique used to make electrodes to bridge the gap between protoplasm and amplifier was devised with the aid of a physical chemist, Dr. Leslie E. Nims, formerly of Yale and now of Brookhaven. Fine silver wire or rod of any suitable dimension is either chlorided by electrolysis in HCl or KCl solution or, following the recommendation of Shedlowsky, is dipped into molten silver chloride which can be obtained at most manufacturing chemists. Usually, it is necessary to make many electrodes and to pair them up so that between any two electrodes there is a minimum of self-potential.

In the early experiments the electrodes were placed in a physiological salt solution in reasonable ionic balance with the salt content of living systems and connected the living protoplasm to the electrode chamber by a salt bridge. For precision work, this is probably the method of choice, but since the magnitudes are in the order of millivolts, the whole procedure can be simplified very considerably by using an inert salt paste.

For this purpose, the Parke-Davis 'Unibase', developed as a foundation for most of the skin creams, can be utilized if, to it, is added sodium chloride. The concentration of sodium chloride in the 'Unibase' paste does not seem to be greatly important for ionic balance between the paste and the protoplasm can be reached in a reasonable time. As a matter of interest, electrodes imbedded in a 'Unibase' salt paste and placed in chambers in contact with the cambium of trees have been used for more than two decades, with considerable success. Most of these electrode placements will remain adequate over long periods of time— weeks and months—but they can be replaced so readily that it is not difficult to continue long-time studies using this technique. Since the type of measurement being made sets the conditions for the type and dimensions of the electrodes, and since the areas to be measured in a living system are limited only by the surface area of the organism, specific directions for making electrodes and electrode chambers can be omitted.

With properly designed electrodes, measurements can be made all over the surface of any living organism from slime mould, through experimental animals, to and including man, with more than adequate reproducibility. The ingenuity of the investigator is the only limit on either the type of electrode to be used or the placement of the electrode. In general, the electrode that is connected to the ground lead of the amplifier is usually put somewhere on the living system at some distance from the area which is being under investigation. The so-called 'hot' electrode, then, is placed as close as common-sense dictates to the area under investigation. What is recorded, therefore, is not specifically a value or a magnitude that is in itself important, but the relationship between any two values measured by the instrument. This makes it clear that we are dealing with relatednesses, rather than absolute magnitude.

It has been known since the time of Willard Gibbs that it is impossible to assign a given magnitude to a potential of any part of the material included between the two electrodes, or to any phase boundary involved between the two electrodes. One can only say as mentioned above, that we are dealing primarily with a difference, a relatedness between the two points under consideration reached by the two electrodes. Most specific phase boundaries can be identified as the source of the voltage gradient. There are innumerable such phase boundaries in any living system, each of which is an adequate source of a voltage gradient. All that we can record is the difference between the potential at one point and that of another point in the living system.

Since we are dealing with relatednesses, the whole point of the technique described here is the change in this relatedness with time. Moreover, since all living systems are individually unique, differing from all other organisms of the same type, each individual system being measured has to serve as its own control. This points again to the importance of change in the relatedness with the passage of time. This does not hold that the potential differences observed are without significance but simply that we are unable with our present techniques to assign a value to a potential difference at any point.

Needless to say, one of the standard questions raised by all this procedure is the source of the potential differences which establish the field in the living system. It is perfectly clear from all that we know about physical chemistry of solutions, even the complex ones of living systems, that the measured electro-motive force is derivable from inherent phase boundaries* to be found whenever two or more states of matter exist side by side.

It must be emphasized, however, that the methods of measurement used in our laboratories over the past thirty years, must be followed rigidly and explicitly. After all, one is balancing electron flow in one vacuum tube against an electron flow in another, in a bridge arrangement. This means that one is dealing

*The term 'phase boundary' designates the line of contact between two dissimilar material substances.

with measuring devices akin to balancing a mercury drop on the point of a needle. In our laboratory, this technique has worked, but it has been clear that unless it is followed certainly and carefully, variations will be found which are inexplicable and which upset the validity of the measurements.

With our 'navigational instruments'—a high impedance amplifier and silver-silver chloride electrodes working through salt bridge in contact with living systems—we have been able to develop a technique which gives reliable results. With this it soon became clear that every living system possesses an electrical field of great complexity. This can be measured with considerable certainty and accuracy and shown to have correlations with growth and development, degeneration and regeneration, and the orientation of component parts in the whole system. Perhaps more interesting that any one thing, this field exhibits remarkable stability through the growth and development of an egg.

It was a basic requirement of this field theory that it be assumed to be a primary characteristic of Nature, in general, and of living systems, in particular. It possesses many, if not all, of the properties necessary to control movement and position of all charged particles within this system. It has those necessary vector or directional properties which are of vital necessity for any understanding of how growth and development can occur under careful, rigid control.

The electrical phenomena associated with the field must be considered to be a primary attribute of Nature, a cause of the arrangement of all the component parts in Nature, not only living but also non-living systems. In other words, the working hypothesis of the studies to be reported here is that the Field is basic with the necessary power and directional properties to determine the processes inherent in the growth and development of any living system.

The field is primary and from it stem all the myriads of consequences which are to be seen in Nature. The specific data which so strongly support this assumption, at least insofar as our present knowledge goes, will be presented in detail in the following pages.

CHAPTER THREE
The Female Field

1

We were ready to set sail. We had developed the navigational instruments and techniques to guide us over uncharted seas towards a hypothetical goal.

But these seas we hoped to explore—the electro-dynamic fields of life—would not yield their secrets if we disturbed them by our passage. So we had to use not a vessel that ploughed through their surface but rather a hovercraft that does not disturb the terrain over which it passes. In other words, our instruments and techniques were designed to measure and map the electro-dynamic fields with the minimum disturbance of their electrical potentials.

With our instruments we could measure the voltage gradients of living systems which are quite independent of changing current and resistance. It must again be emphasized that our measurements are as near as possible pure voltage measurements. To be sure this probably can never be done with absolute accuracy. But, for all practical purposes, in our measurements the current drain from the system being measured is reduced to the minimum. Hence we do not disturb the living system while the measurements are being made. All the necessary energy to keep the instrument in operation or, if you like, our hovercraft hovering, is derived from external sources, not from the system being measured. This is imperative.

The beginning of our voyage is in a land-locked harbour where there is a certain amount of information about the harbour and its surrounding terrain. We know that living systems have electrical properties. Examples are the electro-cardiogram, the electro-encephalogram, the action current potential of nervous impulse, electrical changes which are associated with muscle contraction and, in all probability, the changes which occur during the activity of glandular secretions.

These are all well-recognized phenomena, but so far there has been no general principle which would explain their existence. It has usually been assumed that all these changes in the electrical properties of a living system are the consequence of biological activity. But it is our hunch that a primary electrical field in the living system is responsible. The reason for this should be clear.

When we pick up heart waves and brain waves from living systems the pick-up electrodes are never, or very rarely, in direct contact with the system under measurement. This means there must be some forces in operation which transmit the activity of muscle, or nerve, from the organ itself through the tissues of the body to the electrode wherever it may be. One arm and one leg, in the case of the cardiogram, or on the scalp in the case of the Berger rhythms, or brain waves.

It is generally accepted that the changes in the electro-cardiogram, for example, which can be recorded from one arm and one leg, are the result of some kind of transport, possibly of charged ions. But the fact is clear to anyone who has examined these in detail that the speed of the transmission is far too rapid to be explained by the movement of a charged particle from cardiac muscle to the far-distant leg. The assumption of a field, however, gives an adequate foundation for the recording at the periphery and at some distance, of the phenomena associated with a basic biological property.

With our craft hovering above the surface of the sea, and thereby causing no wash or ripple in the sea itself, we leave the harbour towards the distant buoy. This buoy is an unknown differentiation on the surface of the sea. When we find it we must tackle the question that this discovery poses: Is it really true that *all* biological systems exhibit a significant set of electrical properties?

The first thing to be done, therefore, is to try to determine by measuring of a variety of systems whether there are *always* electro-metric properties in a living organism. So, over the last thirty years, almost every form of living organism has been studied, some of them quite cursorily and others in more detail, from bacteria up to and including man. *And so far as our present information goes, there is unequivocal evidence that wherever there is life, there are electrical properties.*

But again, it must be stressed that these electrical properties, measured under the conditions of this trip, are voltage gradients, not current movement, not changes in resistance to the passage of current.

These electrical voltage gradients in the living systems are the logical consequences of the Electro-dynamic Theory and only to be expected. But we must go beyond theory: its logical consequences must be put to experimental tests to develop what Northrop has called epistemic correlations or what Margenau has called the correspondencies between the logical conclusions from the Theory and the findings in an experimental laboratory where adequate controls can be instituted.

2

If there are electrical gradients—voltage gradients—in living systems, what are their essential characteristics? They must have magnitude and, since they are electrical, they must have directional properties; in other words, polar properties, a positive and a negative aspect.

To learn more about these gradients one of the first things undertaken in the laboratory was—naturally enough—to measure human beings. At first sight, this could be an exceedingly complicated problem, but with the advice of Professor Leslie Nims, a very simple approach was adopted.

With our silver-silver chloride electrodes in a common physiological salt solution, the known self-potential in the electrode was reduced by selection to a minimum, usually not greater than one-half a millivolt. Then with two cups available, one electrode was introduced into the salt solution of one cup and another electrode into the salt solution of a second cup. It was a simple matter, then, to dip the finger of the hands into these cups; the index finger of the left hand into the left-hand cup, and the index finger of the right hand into the right-hand cup. This completed the external circuit in the measuring device.

Immediately it was clear that there was a voltage gradient between the left finger and the right finger. This could be checked readily, for all that was necessary was to move the right-hand finger into the left-hand cup and vice versa. If the readings were valid, the magnitude should be the same in the second series of measurements as in the first. Normally, with our experiments these measurements were repeated ten times, or until we had reproducible, reliable results.

As soon as it was found that such measurements could be made readily, the question arose whether there was any significant difference between human beings and those measurements. As a result a great many measurements were carried out in the laboratory, using the personnel of the laboratory as subjects. We found to our delight that the magnitudes of the potentials were rarely less than two millivolts and often many times higher.

The spread—or magnitude—of the measurements was so great that it was found possible to divide human beings into four categories. Individuals with low voltage gradients between the right and left forefinger; at the other extreme, individuals with voltage gradients between the right and left forefinger of something in the order of ten millivolts. In between, there was a third group, a low-high group, around five or six millivolts, and a fourth high-low group around two to four millivolts.

Interestingly enough, these were quite consistent during the period of measurement but, what is more remarkable, they were quite consistent with the passage of time. These experiments were carried out over many days to be sure that the results were reliable. If the electrical gradients in the living system were the result of the chemistry of the organism, the constancy which we recorded would simply not be possible.

We could not see any significant relationships between the individuals with low potential gradients and those with high potential gradients by any techniques which we were able to devise. The subjects were all males, and it was suggested that there might be an electrical difference between males and females. Hence, measurements were made on female members of the labor-

48

atory group, day after day, week after week, and month after month.

We found to our astonishment that during the course of a month's measurements the female voltage gradients showed remarkable increases, a sharp rise, for a period of twenty-four hours. This occurred on many occasions and gave us reason to wonder as to the possible origin of this phenomenon. Examination of the personal records of the females involved made it clear that these rises in voltage gradient occurred during the approximate middle of the menstrual cycle. Needless to say, this suggested at once that the rise might be associated with ovulation, since the endocrinologists have been telling us for years that ovulation occurs in the middle of the menstrual cycle and is, in all probability, the cause of the onset of the menses.

3

This was an exciting event, for now we could see beyond the first buoy a second buoy in the distance: *a change in voltage gradient associated with fundamental biological activity.* Attention must be called, however, to the fact that the change was one of magnitude, not of the polarity of the measurements.

Since not all mammals have the same history, it was necessary to seek an animal in which the time of ovulation could be predicted. Fortunately, the rabbit is such an animal. Proper stimulation of the cervix in the female rabbit results, under normal conditions, in the appearance of ovulation some nine hours after stimulus.

The following experiment, therefore, was set up: A rabbit was stimulated, and nine hours later anaesthetized. Its abdomen was then opened and a salt-filled chamber was placed around the ovary. The cold electrode was attached to the animal's body, and the 'hot' electrode, connected to the grid of the first tube, was placed in the salt-filled chamber not too far away from the ovary itself. Then, with a microscope, the surface of the ovary was itself continuously examined while the changes in voltage gradient between the two electrodes were recorded on the recording galvanometer. It was thus possible to see the event of ovulation through the microscope and, simultaneously, the recorded changes in voltage gradient on the recorder.

To our delight *the moment of rupture of the follicle and the release of the egg was accompanied by a sharp change in the voltage gradient on the electrical recorder.* This experiment was carried out enough times until it was perfectly clear that there could be little or no question that the electrical change was associated with the event of ovulation.

If, in an experimental animal, electrical changes were seen to coincide with ovulation, then it might be possible to assume that the observed voltage-gradients in women might serve to time ovulation in human beings. This is a very important problem, for the exact time when eggs are released from the human ovary has not been really determined. As these voltage gradients occur during the middle of a menstrual cycle then, if the Knaus theory is correct, ovulation occurs in the middle of the cycle, and therefore the electrical changes in the human female should indicate the time of ovulation in that particular individual.

This is not an easy experiment to perform on humans but, through a fortunate set of circumstances, it was possible for us to do a study on one girl. It was necessary for her to have an elective laparotomy and she was willing to come into the hospital and have the operation performed at a time when our electrical records indicated that it was the right time to do it. She was in the hospital for fifty-six hours before the operation and during that time was continuously measured by the recording galvanometer. There were times, of course, when short gaps occurred in the record for a variety of physiological reasons, but the fact remains that there was a rather astonishing consistency in the electric measurements.

The measurements were made between the central abdominal wall, as a reference electrode, and the wall of the vagina in the vicinity of the cervix, as the active electrode. When the electrical records showed this marked change in voltage gradient in the patient, she was moved to the operating room and, under the skillful hands of Dr. Luther Musselman, a laparotomy was performed, an ovary uncovered, and a recently ruptured follicle noted. This, obviously confirmed the findings in the rabbit.

4

At this point occurred one of the most interesting events of this adventure in science:

Dr. John Rock, of Brookline, Massachusetts, head of a gynaecological hospital, evinced interest in the techniques and undertook to develop the procedures in his hospital. We gave him all the advice and help that we could, and eventually he set up a number of measurements at that hospital. He reported in a paper some ten or more instances of ovulation occurring in the middle of the menstrual cycle as indicated by electrical measurements. He completed these experiments, or at least the first of them, however, before we had been able to find a suitable patient for our work in New Haven. Like the gentleman he is, he withheld publication of his findings until after we were able to publish ours. Subsequently, he continued these experiments and confirmed our original findings.

An accident occurred, however, when a house officer inadvertently made some measurements on a female patient not in the middle of the menstrual cycle. He found to his dismay—and that of the rest of the observers—that *these electro-metric changes did not always come in the middle of the cycle.*

It will be recalled that the Knaus theory holds that ovulation occurs in the middle of the menstrual cycle. This theory was based on statistical measure of pregnancies following returning soldiers during the first World War; and there is probably little question that the statistics are valid so far as *groups* are concerned. Unfortunately, that does not demonstrate beyond peradventure that in every *individual* ovulation must necessarily occur in the middle of the menstrual cycle. Dr. Rock felt, however, that the statistical evidence was valid; and therefore any changes in electro-metrics of the living patient, not in the middle of the cycle, could not be related to ovulation. This terminated

Dr. Rock's experiment, much to our dismay, but we persisted, nevertheless, in our study.

With the help of Dr. Dorothy Barton, an extended study was made of a group of women in the New Haven Hospital, most of whom were nurses living a fairly rigorous existence, with more regularity than most of us undergo. These women included subjects of all ages. Some of them were post-menopausal.

One of the interesting consequences of this study was the fact that about thirty per cent of the women seemed to ovulate in the middle of the cycle, granting the validity of the electro-metric technique. But in all probability—according to electrical measurements—two-thirds of the women ovulated over the entire menstrual cycle, even during the menses. This was at variance with the endocrinological theory of ovulation and was difficult for many people to accept.

Women over the menstrual period and in the non-fertile period and those in the so-called menopause, showed no such electro-metric changes with the passage of time. This was true whether the menopause was the natural one or one resulting from surgery of the generative tract.

For a number of years measurements were made on patients, sent in by surrounding doctors, to time ovulation in their particular instances. One of the patients sent to us was one who had been married for a number of years without issue. The question was raised, of course, as to the reason for the infertility. Though all the known techniques of that time were employed no significant fact was uncovered to explain why there was no fertile result.

The patient was taught to make the measurements herself and did them religiously once a day, day-after-day, for many months. At no time was there any evidence of voltage variations. Subsequently, when a laparotomy was required, it was found that the patient had atrophied ovaries, apparently caused by their early involvement in tuberculosis. At no time had she ovulated and there were no electro-metric changes.

This raises the question of the necessarily causal relationship between ovulation and the onset of menstruation. In the group of patients studied, moreover, while the great majority showed fairly regular menstrual periods of the average length, there were a number whose menstrual histories were very irregular. One patient in particular exhibited menstruation only three times in a year, and yet during that year there were three instances where there was a marked electro-metric change unrelated to the onset of menstruation itself and suggested that ovulation had occurred.

The evidence is clear. Like brain waves and heart waves, electro-metric changes occur during ovulation and can be recorded in the living subject. Furthermore, the results show that ovulation may take place at any time in the menstrual cycle, although in the majority of women studied the ovulation record showed the usual mid-cycle peak. It is equally clear that there is no necessary relationship between ovulation and menstruation, for either may exist without the other; ovulation may occur without menstruation and menses without ovulation.

5

Published reports of our experiments with women were read by the distinguished obstetrician and gynaecologist, Dr. Louis Langman, of New York University and Bellevue Hospital. As a result, he came to the writer's laboratory and discussed the question of whether or not the electro-metric timing of ovulation could be used in connection with artificial insemination. Moreover, because the reports indicated that electro-metric records suggested relationship between the developing ovaries and its follicle, he further questioned whether or not they might not be used to detect cancer. The result was a rewarding and very fruitful association over a number of years.

Starting with the assumption that the electro-metric peaks occurring during the menstrual cycle of normal women indicated ovulation, Dr. Langman decided to use the technique as a means of determining when best to employ artificial insemination. As a result, he was equipped with the necessary technical apparatus, including the electrode, the high input impedance amplifier and the G. E. photoelectric recorder.

Since Dr. Langman had had indifferent success in a series of ten cases, using other timing procedures, artificial insemination was attempted in those instances when the electro-metric shift indicated that ovulation had recently occurred. To his and our delight, the average of successes was considerably higher using the electro-metric technique than that employed by other methods of timing ovulation.

It seemed clear, however, that Dr. Langman's main interest was not only in the timing of ovulation, but also in the problem of malignancy in the generative tract in women.

Fortunately, through a grant, and with the cooperation of the Bellevue Hospital Gynaecological Service, more than a hundred patients were examined electro-metrically. The records were kept carefully and a marked voltage gradient between cervix of the uterus and a reference electrode on the ventral abdominal wall often appeared on the recording galvanometer.

After a sufficient number of tests had been run to make sure we were dealing with a valid finding, Dr. Langman and his assistant examined something in the neighbourhood of one thousand patients. These patients were on the wards of the hospital and were subject to a variety of syndromes. They included fibromas, as well as the usual run of pathological events in the generative tract of these women. In those that showed a marked change in the voltage gradient between the cervix and the ventral abdominal wall, careful watch was kept through subsequent laparotomy.

There were a hundred and two cases where there was a significant shift in the voltage gradient, suggesting malignancy. *Surgical confirmation was found in ninety-five of the hundred and two cases.*

The actual position of the malignancy varied all the way from the fundus, to the tubes and to the ovarian tissue itself. It is interesting to note that the electro-metric evidence of sharp voltage change occurred in malignancies found not only in the immediate vicinity of the cervix but also through all the rest of the generative tract, including the ovary itself. Thus we had an astonishingly high percentage of successful identification of malignancy in the generative tract, confirmed by biopsy.

The fact that malignancy in the ovarian tissue was recognized electro-metrically, and confirmed by biopsy—even though the malignant tissue was several centimetres distant from the active electrode in contact with the cervix—is in line with the distant readings of the EKG and EEG. The order of magnitude of these changes in voltage gradient was such that the possibility of changing pH of the generative tract could be ruled out.

Surprisingly enough, these findings were never picked up in the literature and have not been extended further cr repeated under other conditions. This probably is because it is difficult for people to recognize that these changes represent changes in the *field* of the system; and, therefore—as in the case of the EKG and the EEG—the active electrode need not be in direct contact with the tissue which is showing the greatest changes in voltage gradient.

It took over thirty years before the EKG was perfected to the point where it could become a useful adjunct in the clinician's office. By that time the empirical results were so clear-cut that the value of the electro-cardiogram could not be questioned. The explanation of EKG, however, has never been really unravelled satisfactorily. The fact that the electrodes do not have to be in contact with the heart, that the change is exceedingly rapid and cannot be explained by electro-phoresis or any of the other simple answers to the transmission of changes of voltage gradient, was finally ignored because of the value of the empirical results.

Similarly, in the case of the electrical ovulation changes and the malignancy changes in the generative tract of women, it is not necessary for the electrode to be in direct contact with the tissue showing the great change. But the voltage-change is transmitted over a distance promptly and in such a form that at present the only successful explanation is that the electrometric characters of tissue, in general, and of the generative tract, in particular, are transmitted by the primary electrodynamic field.

6

The results reported above suggested that the relationship between ovulation and menstruation was not on quite such a firm foundation as had been generally assumed. There can be no question that the chemistry of the endocrines is an important factor in these activities of the generative tract. Primarily, however, the chemistry provides the energy necessary for these activities, and it has been almost entirely overlooked that the chemistry involved in any physiological process must, necessarily, have direction.

The source of this direction can be assumed safely to be the result of the activity of the nervous system and there is plenty of evidence in the literature to suggest that in the hypothalamic region of the brain there are nuclear masses which are concerned primarily with the onset of ovulation, its completion and, also, that another set of neural mechanisms has equal control over the menstrual cycle.

While experiments on ovulation in humans were going on, parallel studies were carried out on experimental animals. With the co-operation of the distinguished gynaecologist, Dr. Luther Musselman, also Dr. Dorothy Barton, Dr. John Boling, and Dr. Vincent Gott, and numerous patient and cooperative subjects, studies were carried out on rats, in particular, on rabbits, cats, and so on. Various stages in the oestrous cycle in animals were found to have electro-metric correlates which are valuable indicators of the kind of physiological processes which are going on during menstruation, and during the whole cycle of oestrous phenomena. In addition to the original findings on the rabbit, Dr. Gott, in particular, extended them to the ovulation phenomena in monkeys.

As a result of the very generous cooperation of Dr. Gertrude Van Wagenen, it was possible for Dr. Gott to study the ovulation problem in a group of Rhesus females. Five animals, for a total of twelve menstrual cycles, were studied. It was found that in ten out of twelve cycles there was a significant and consistent peak of negative voltage that was higher than any other peak in the cycle and, because of its distinctive pattern, may be distinguished from any other peaks in the cycle. This distinctive peak occurred in every cycle between the eleventh and fourteenth day, and this is the period in which most of the ovulations are known to occur. It is believed that this distinctive and reproducible peak is the electrical concomitant of ovulation.

Possibly the two cycles without a significant peak, between the eleventh and fourteenth days, are anovulatory cycles which are fairly common in the monkey. Bi-weekly or weekly records of the abdominal vaginal potential difference were made in two monkeys from the date of conception until delivery six months later. In other animals, records were taken from the second month of pregnancy to the date of delivery.

The records tend to level out somewhat as pregnancy proceeds, so that by the third month the graph is almost a horizontal line. The cervix remains negative after the second week of pregnancy until the beginning of the third month, except for rare instances when it becomes positive. By the third month, the voltage has dropped to near the zero line where it hovers until delivery.

Despite these characteristics which differentiate pregnancy from the menstrual cycle, there are no significant and consistent changes during the first month of pregnancy that might permit the detection of pregnancy a few days after conception.

These results, together with the findings of Dr. John Boling in the oestrous cycle of the rat, make it quite clear that electro-metrics of the field characteristics of the living organism can provide useful information about the whole physiology of the generative tract.

Since all of these experiments stemmed from the basic assumption that the living organism possesses an electro-dynamic field as a whole, with constituent and subsidiary parts or local fields, which are specific components of the living system, the well-controlled experimental findings confirmed the general validity of the primary assumption.

Any individual component of the whole system has, of course, its own characteristic field which is a part of the field of the whole organism. Any variations which may occur can be assumed to be variations in the flow of energy in the system, a flow of energy which arises first of all in chemistry and is controlled and directed by the electro-dynamic field of the whole organism.

7

The experiments which had shown the positive correlation between the electro-metrics of the generative tract in women and the presence of malignancy throughout the tract led at once to a further examination of the possibility of electro-metric correlates of malignancy elsewhere.

In the growth and development of every living system there is obviously some kind of control of the processes. In the midst of incredibly complex flux, direction is available for the control of this growth and for differentiation. As a distinguished zoologist once said, 'The growth and development of any living system would appear to be controlled by someone sitting "on the organism" and directing its whole living process.'

One of the few things we know of in the Universe that has direction are the electrical properties of things, in general. The Field Theory suggested that it should be possible to determine the polarity and direction of the flow of energy transformations in the living system. The organism, as a whole, depends on such directives for its continued existence; *so also does atypical growth.*

Energy, however, is a basic requirement, indifferent to the direction in which it flows. It is important, therefore, to realize that in the development of growth and development of the organism there are forces in addition to the undirected properties of chemical changes, factors which give direction to the flow of energy.

It cannot be denied that morphogenesis is directed. This is true of the whole organism and also of its constituent parts. Moreover, the very direction of development implies a necessary relationship between the units of which the system is composed, a relationship which imparts to the organism that quality which makes the whole greater than the sum of its parts.

Considerations such as these led to an examination of the electrical properties of cancer-susceptible mice. The experiments were designed to determine whether or not the polarity vectors were altered in atypical growth.

Through the courtesy of Dr. L. C. Strong and Dr. G. M. Smith, a considerable number of mice from the colonies of Dr. Strong, were studied weekly. There were four groups of such mice: A. normal control, B. a strain of mice known to have a high incidence of mammary cancer occurring spontaneously, C. a strain of mice prone to atypical growth following the administration of carcinogens, and D. a number of mice from a strain which readily accepted implanted malignant tissue.

Comparison of the groups made it clear that statistically the control group showed a different electrical pattern from that found in the animals with spontaneous breast cancer, malignancy produced by carcinogens, or the atypical growth of transplants. There were also statistically significant differences between spontaneous carcinogenics and the transplanted growth. While day-by-day variations in both magnitude and polarity occurred there was sufficient variability to make it difficult to show a direct one-to-one relationship for any individual animal. Clearly enough, there are other factors in the presence of atypical growth responsible for the variability.

To carry out an experiment it is necessary to control conditions of food, water, and temperature. A few preliminary experiments indicated that the individual variability could be reduced significantly. All the evidence so far collected makes it necessary to study them under more controlled laboratory conditions.

Through the generous cooperation of Dr. H. S. N. Greene, some three hundred mice were intensively studied following the implantation in the breast region of the C38 strain of mice. The implantations were made by Dr. Greene in the right axilla. They were from malignant tissue labelled 4578B-PXB-PX and MTH. In addition, foetal and visceral implants were made from normal animals.

Measurements were made between the right axilla and the left axilla in unanaesthetized mice. The common reference point for the potential differences between the axillae was the placement of an electrode in the mouth of the animal. Since the left side of the animal was not involved in implantation, it served to some extent as a control for the operated side.

The results of the experiment were surprisingly consistent.

Twenty-four to twenty-eight hours after the implantation changes were to be observed in the voltage gradients. This difference increased steadily and quite smoothly to reach a maximum of approximately five millivolts on or about the eleventh day, following which it decreased.

In the animals with the foetal implant representing, therefore, a rapidly growing mass of embryonic tissue, the difference began to appear a little later, and reached a peak on approximately the sixth day, following which the potential difference dropped to zero and reversed its polarity until the end of the experiment.

In the slow-growing tumours potential differences began to emerge on the third or fourth day but reached their maximum of approximately three millivolts on the tenth or eleventh day. From there, until the end of the experiment, the differences in potential fell steadily to zero. The control, and those without growth, showed a variable between the two sides of less than a millivolt for the entire experiment. In all of these measurements, the axilla containing the implanted foreign material was negative to the opposite axillary region.

It is clear from these findings that the crest of atypical growth in the host organism produced measurable and reproducible electro-metric correlates. The rapidly growing tumours developed higher potentials more quickly than the slow-growing implant. The foetal tissue started off rather promptly but early reached an electro-metric peak and thereafter declined to zero, subsequently to appear as a polar reversal which, in turn, returned to zero. The slow-growing implants started late but exhibited an electro-metric curve paralleling the essential slope of the rapidly growing tumours, but reached their lower maximum at approximately the same time as the rapidly growing tumours.

These experiments on mice, of course, offered valuable confirmation of our findings that atypical voltage-gradients in the fields of women are associated with malignancy.

CHAPTER FOUR
The Ubiquitous Field

1

While we were carrying out experiments on men and women we were also exploring the electro-dynamic fields in other forms of life because we wanted to assure ourselves that these fields are a universal property of all living forms and are not confined to the higher forms of life.

We explored the fields of a frog's eggs—as mentioned in the first chapter—not only to satisfy ourselves that something so small and relatively simple possessed a field but also to find support for our theory that the field controls the growth and development of the form.

Using micro-pipettes filled with salt solution and connected to the voltmeter we found different voltage gradients across different axes of the eggs. We marked the axis of the largest voltage gradient with spots of Nile blue sulphate and later found, as the eggs developed, that the frog's nervous system always grew along the axis with the highest voltage gradient. This was an indication that the field is primary—the matrix that shapes the living form.

Next we looked for a living system with some unquestioned design or pattern, the field of which could be examined through growth and development. The nervous system of a vertebrate offers a pattern which can be analysed and which, we hoped, would yield some clues to the nature of the forces or laws which determine the pattern.

Our choice fell on salamanders for our experimental animals because they are easily obtained and can be observed from the egg stage up to adult form; and the changes in the form as it grows and develops can be observed and described with great accuracy.

Amphibia, too, are admirably suited to the experimental analysis of the growth and development of the nervous system. They are vertebrates and, therefore, have a head and tail axis, a bilateral symmetry, a right side and a left side, a dorsal and ventral side. This is the most elementary aspect of the pattern of organization of the vertebrate nervous system.

Moreover, by using microsurgical methods, it is possible to perform operations on the nervous system, to remove parts of it and to observe the consequences to its development. Pieces can be transplanted from one part of the nervous system to another in order to examine the results.

Finally, salamanders are easily raised in the laboratory, with no serious problems of care. No anaesthetics are necessary and they are abundant in the spring of the year.

We were reinforced in our choice of salamanders by the evidence, slowly increasing over the years, that they possess certain electrical properties.

2

We started with numerous experiments on the developing embryos of salamanders, because an analysis of the embryology of the nervous system promised data to support our Field Theory.

In the first place, as the embryo is an aquatic animal, it was necessary to determine whether or not there were any significant electro-metrics of the embryo. Potential measurements were made, therefore, in the embryo from a point in the cephalic region, and another in the caudal region. These were studied over periods of time and showed characteristic changes with the growth and differentiating of the embryo itself.

It soon became clear that there is an electro-metric correlate of the longitudinal axis of the salamander nervous system. There is also a bilateral symmetry between the right side and the left side of the axis, as might be expected from everything else we know about the developing organism.

To run down this problem a little further, measurements were made of the unfertilized egg of a salamander, using the animal pole as a reference point, and a moving electrode around the equator of the egg in the four quadrants of the development. It is well known, of course, that the salamander egg at this stage is a sphere, showing little or no differentiation grossly except the difference between the animal and vegital pole. But there is no differentiation, so far as can be observed, in the quadrants of the sphere. Measurements were made, therefore, in the unfertilized egg between the north, or animal pole, and four points on the equator.

It was found from these measurements that there was one point on the equator which showed a marked increase in the voltage drop between the reference electrode and the point. The latter was marked with a spot of Nile blue sulphate so that it could be followed through the subsequent period of development. It was found—as our theory had suggested—that the point on the equator which marked the greatest voltage drop from the animal pole marked the head end of the developing salamander.

A longitudinal axis of the developing nervous system was then established in the *unfertilized* egg. This maintained itself throughout the succeeding growth period and, surprisingly enough, there was no significant change in the electro-metrics of the unfertilized egg after fertilization.

This is astonishing, because fertilization is supposed to be a critical point in development. But apparently—in the salamander, at least—the electric field properties of the egg are established quite independently not only of the fact of fertilization but also of the plane of ingress of the sperm head into the egg. This suggests, at once, that the design of the living embryo is an electro-metric correlate which can be recorded objectively during the process of growth and development and turns out to be one of the constant factors during this whole process of development.

One of the strange things about development that has always been known is the extraordinary constancy in which the direction of development moves. As a distinguished friend of mine once said, 'The growth and development of an embryo would seem to be the result of the fact that some kind of a factor sits on the embryo during its entire development and gives direction to it.' From the evidence at hand, up to date, it would seem fairly obvious that the one constant factor in growth and development—which include not only the increase in the numbers of cells, but also their differentiation—is the field of the organism.

All these measurements were made using silver-silver chloride electrodes immersed in micropipettes and connected to the high input impedance of a suitable amplifier with a galvanometer or a recording galvanometer in the output. At the suggestion of one of my early colleagues, Dr. Leslie F. Nims, now at Brookhaven Laboratories, on Long Island, it was noticed that as the micropipette electrodes were pulled away from the surface of the embryo, a voltage gradient could still be recorded. In fact, drop-off of voltage gradient carried on as far as one or one and a half millimetres from the embryo.

This is truly extraordinary, for it makes it clear that *the field properties of the embryo radiate through the medium of the liquid environment in which the embryo lives.*

Now this could occur only if the source of these potential gradients was the result of field activity. As a matter of fact, if one stops to think about it, if one puts a battery of any kind in a conducting medium, the battery very soon is exhausted, since the external medium acts as a low resistance shunt across the positive and negative poles of the battery. But in the embryo, although we have the same kind of voltage gradient as is present in the battery—at least so far as the measurable characteristics are concerned—nevertheless *the field properties of the embryo do not short out in the liquid.*

These experiments led to a further analysis of the field properties. It was suggested that if an embryo were rotated mechanically underneath two micropipette electrodes, there should be a constant rise and fall in voltage gradient as the head and tail axis of the embryo passed underneath the micropipette electrode. This experiment was set up with a mechanically revolving stage on which was placed a half-grown salamander embryo and the recorded output of the high input impedance amplifier transmitted to a G-E photoelectric recording galvanometer.

The result was extraordinary, for there was a sine wave output from the revolving embryo, the frequency of which, of course, was a function of the speed with which the embryo revolved. Moreover, it was clear that the field axis was a constant to the whole procedure and resulted in a very interesting sine wave output from the embryo itself. This meant, too, that the micropipette electrodes were recording voltage gradients well away from the embryo itself.

As a control, an inert glass rod was revolved under the same experimental conditions and produced a straight line on the recording galvanometer. To make a further check, a 'robot' was made of a piece of copper rod with a blob of solder at one end. Such a rod, under normal conditions, produces a voltage gradient, because of the bi-metallic components. This also was revolved in the same way as the embryo and produced the same kind of sine wave, the only difference being that, in time, the bi-metallic chemical voltage gradient decreased.

Similar experiments were made with a full-grown salamander floated in a circular dish of salt solution in which, at opposite ends of a diameter, were immersed the electrodes, connected to a recording galvanometer.

The dish was then slowly rotated and, since the salamander possessed a field with a positive and negative pole, it acted like the armature of an electrical generator. In consequence, as it rotated between the electrodes, it set up a tiny alternating current of very low frequency, which was recorded as a true sine wave.

One day, perhaps, some enterprising experimenter will float a man or a woman in a rotating swimming-pool to demonstrate that there really is such a thing as a 'human dynamo'! But the author's laboratory offered neither space nor facilities for such an experiment.

3

The experiments described above made it clear that, using proper electro-metric techniques, recorded voltage gradients without current drain from the system measured are a valid expression of the basic, primary electro-dynamic field. Since the experiments also indicated that direct contact with the living organism was not necessary to measure a voltage gradient, a rigorously-controlled experiment was set up, using the sciatic nerve of a frog, with the help of another colleague, Dr. Alexander Mauro, now at the Rockefeller Institute in New York. This experiment was designed to explore the field properties of a small part of a living system.

The beautifully-precise formulation by Lorente de Nó of fields in an infinite-volume conductor accompanying the neural impulse, travelling along the sciatic nerve of the frog, demanded that a search be made for experimental evidence of the existence of a quasi-electrostatic field in the air surrounding a nerve trunk.

A preliminary report of such a study is here presented. The existence of an electro-static field has been demonstrated. However, an analysis of the nature of this field is far from complete and much further study will be required.

By an ingenious technique developed by Dr. Mauro, the results of the activity of the sciatic nerve of the frog were studied, using a thousand-megohm input-impedance preamplifier, followed by suitable amplifiers with an output to a cathode-ray tube. It was possible to study the transmission of a single stimulus throughout the substance of the segment of the nerve under study, not only when the electrodes were in direct contact, but also when they were at a measurable distance outside the nerve.

The evidence resulting from these experiments gives further enlightenment as to the nature of the field in living systems. It is becoming increasingly clear that these fields are in fact quasi-electro-static fields. Originally, the term 'electro-dynamic field' was used to describe, in the most general way, the nature of the fields in living organisms, but it is now possible to give a more precise definition. Measurement of such fields indicates that *forces exist not only in but also outside of the nerve during excitation.*

Thus, to the study of steady state parameters of these fields that have been recorded in amphibia and—as we shall see—plants, must be added these records of the changing properties of electrical fields in association with biologic activity. To be sure, the EEG and the EKG are instances of the same phenomenon and in a sense the observations recorded here are no more than might be expected. All of them are the direct consequences of field properties of living systems.

None of this implies that the field is conceived of as some mysterious property of living things. It is not another name for *elan vital* or entelechy. It is a definable concept capable of precise measurement and is to be thought of in the same terms as fields in the non-living Universe.

Electric fields in physics are not only widely accepted, but technologies based upon them have been extraordinarily productive. In non-living matter, fields are definable in terms of forces between charges. They are, in part, a measure of the relationships between entities. In living systems, therefore, since the entities of which they are composed are the same entities as are to be found in non-living matter, the same forces between the units may be presumed. The basic difference between the two lies in the enormously increased complexity of the necessary relatednesses in living organisms.

It would seem reasonable to assume, therefore, that the relationship of entities in living organisms may be measured by field properties just as successfully as in atoms or between atoms.

It should be noted that the electro-static fields do not exist in the absence of charges nor charges in the absence of fields. They are both fundamental properties of matter. In living organisms it can be said that chemical components, wherever they possess charges, cannot exist without fields nor can fields be found except in the presence of charges.

It is equally clear that the business of living is not a static affair; it is a moving, dynamic process. For this energy is required and it is the chemistry of biological systems which provides it. But energy is a scalar property and is, itself, indifferent to the direction in which it flows. In general, it is the second law of thermodynamics which directs the flow in such a manner as to increase the entropy of the system.

It seems from our observations that this direction is also characterized by electrical gradients, much as though the second law was augmented by electrical signposts. Moreover, these electrical signs have an astonishing constancy in spite of the enormously complex chemical flux. Such constancy of directional control, in fact, is one of the striking attributes of the developing organism. Quasi-electro-static fields, although changing slowly, persist in time and can, perhaps to some approximation, be conceived as providing the necessary direction.

The experiments reported by us in collaboration with Dr. Mauro provide additional evidence of the validity of the original assumption.

4

Pursuing our exploration of fields in widely-different living forms, we made a study of the voltage-gradients in the marine animal, Obelia, a polyp. These experiments were carried out through the courtesy of the late Dr. F. S. Hammett, of the Marine Experimental Station of the Lankenau Hospital Research Institute. They were made on animals collected at the experimental station at Truro on Cape Cod.

A series of measurements of the voltage gradients of definitive stages in the life cycle of an Obelia hybrid was carried out. These trace a rising curve of graded intensity parallel with the growth from the anlagen to the complete functioning animal. The values reach their peak in the feeding animal and then drop off as regression to the senile state begins. With the attainment of senility and its consequent catabolic dissolution the direction of the voltage gradient is reversed.

Fluctuations in voltage gradient parallel the fluctuations in developmental growth, as it progresses from an undifferentiated to the differentiated state. The conclusion was made that the growth and life cycle of an Obelia is characterized by definitive and progressive changes in voltage gradient correlated with the morphogenesis of the animal. There are a number of implications of this study which deserve further examination.

In the extremely short life-cycle of Obelia it is possible to cover the entire life span of the living organism in a relatively short time. During the early growth and differentiation of the animal, increasing voltage gradients were recorded until a peak was reached at the time when the animal was fully developed and feeding.

As is well-known, after this the activity of the animal begins to decline and a regression occurs with senility until the so-called death of the particular hydranth. The electro-metric correlates of this regression were clearly evident.

This tends to confirm some observations made in the study of mice that there is a fairly regular pattern of growth and development up to the eventual death of the living system. During the first third of the animal's life, voltage gradients increase fairly steadily. During the middle third, voltage gradients tend to level off and form a plateau. The last third of an animal's life shows evidence of regression with a consequent falling off of voltage gradients until death itself ensues.

All of these experiments show a relationship between the growth and development of a living system and its electro-metric correlates. One of the important consequences of the field theory, however, is that the electro-metric characteristics of the system in some way control the pattern of organization or, if you like, the design of the system.

5

With the generous co-operation of the late Professor Edmund W. Sinnott, a study was made of the electrical patterns in cucurbits. In this field, Dr. Sinnott, an expert, has called attention to the fact that the shape of gourds is not a function of the morphological characteristics of the cellular components. The cucurbits all have a characteristic building block, and yet the shape of the gourd made with these building blocks differs. Just as one can build a house with bricks of a uniform size and shape, the design of the whole results in quite different external characteristics.

Using cucurbit fruits, provided by Dr. Sinnott, electro-metrics were made. In this study, potential differences were measured along the axial and the equitorial diameters of young ovaries and developing fruits of three races of *cucurbita pepo*, differing markedly in shape and designated as elongated, round, and flat.

The size of the potential differences bears little relation to the absolute size of the dimensions along which they occur, but the ratio of the potential differences is closely correlated with the ratio of the dimensions.

As the fruit grow larger, the potential gradients tend in all races to decrease, but the ratios between the gradients and the true dimensions tend to increase in the elongate, to decrease in the flat, and to be unchanged in the round race.

To explain these various facts, it is tempting to suggest that the pattern of potential differences here described may have some causal relation to the morphological pattern which appears as the fruit develops. The evidence here presented is in entire agreement with that obtained in animal material and may be interpreted in the same way. The data offers for the consideration of students of plant morphogenesis a series of new facts from a field which, if well cultivated, may become very fruitful.

The association with Professor Sinnott was extraordinarily fruitful. Many suggestions were made as to the kind of electrometric studies which could be made on growing systems. Two of these were furthered. The first of these, following Professor Sinnott, was carried out with the help of Oliver Nelson, at that time a student in the Graduate School of Yale University, Department of Botany, and closely associated with the Connecticut Agricultural Experiment Station. The suggestion was made that electro-metric studies be made of a single seed. The choice was necessitated largely by practical considerations and fell on corn kernels—sweet corn kernels.

With the co-operation of the Connecticut Agricultural Experiment Station, it became possible to study the electrical patterns in several pure and hybrid strains of sweet corn. These seeds had been under study for some time. The strains differ considerably in genetic constitution and in the degree of hybrid vigour shown in crosses between them. Four inbred strains were studied and three hybrids. One of these was a mid-season yellow sweet corn, an inbred of unknown origin. Another was a semi-dwarf mutant of P-39; it is normal in appearance but much reduced in size. It has been shown by Singleton that they differ by only one gene.

In this material, therefore, we had four stable pure strains of significantly different properties with which to correlate electrical patterns. The three hybrids show a gradation of hybrid vigour. If the electrical patterns have any significance, the electrical correlates of these differences should be manifest. A statistical analysis shows that the mean potential measured between the attached end of the corn kernel and its opposite pole gave highly significant results.

Aside from the generally different mean, however, the most striking finding was a very great difference between the mean of the single gene mutant and the parent stock. It is remarkable that the change of a single gene in the parent stock should produce such profound and significant change in the over-all pattern of the voltage difference. The conclusion seems to be inescapable that there is a very close relationship between the genetic constitution and the electrical pattern. If further studies should confirm this conclusion, it seems very probable that one of the ways the chromosomes impart design to protoplasm is through the medium of an electro-dynamic field.

In these studies of voltage gradients in maize kernels, the longitudinal gradient between the germinal end and the micropolar end of the seed was used as a test measurement. Under the conditions of the experiment there appeared to be, first of all, an immediate potential, which was called the prime potential. Moments after this prime potential was determined, the voltage gradient nearly always dropped to a much lower value and remained remarkably stable for the minutes during which the observations were made.

The prime potentials apparently show a high correlation with the seeds' viability, but have no particular reference to plant growth. The equilibrium potential, on the other hand, is not correlated with seed viability but rather with the inherent genetic constitution of a plant, since by use of the potentiometer and equilibrium potential determinations, one can *segregate from a given population those seeds with superior growth characteristics.* Further, these potential differences between seeds have been highly correlated with the growth of progeny for one generation removed. For these reasons the potentiometer may prove to be a useful tool for the plant breeder.

Electro-metric data from maize seeds show remarkable correlation with growth potentials in the corn kernel, as well as a significant relationship to genetic constitution. These findings raise the old question of which is more important, the genetic constitution of a living system, or the environment in which it lives?

6

As a contribution to this problem, a study was made of the reactions to a stimulus of the sensitive plant, Mimosa. It is well known, of course, that a branch will collapse when touched. Its electrical correlates, therefore, at the collapse of the branch provide a clue as to the importance of the changing physical environment of a living system and its electrical correlates.

It is well known, too, that in all biological systems there exists a multiplicity of phase boundaries. The existence of a potential difference across the phase boundaries is generally accepted. It is commonly held that the membrane potential at a phase boundary is a consequence of a difference in concentrations of electrolytes on opposite sides of the boundary. In the non-living system this potential approaches zero as ionic equilibrium is reached. It has been more or less logically concluded, therefore, that the existence and variation of potential difference can be explained by the known initial differences in concentrations with consequent movement of ions across the boundary.

The living system, on the other hand, differs somewhat from the physical chemical situation in that the potential differences, instead of approaching zero with time, are maintained at an astonishingly stable level. The maintenance of this level of potential difference presupposes constant recruitment and it is natural to assume that this recruitment comes in large measure from chemical activity. Moreover, it is not at all impossible that one of the mechanisms regulating and controlling chemical activity is resident in the potential difference.

In other words, if this problem is looked at from a slightly different angle, it is legitimate to make the assumption that in a living system the total energy intake appears, in part, in the chemical flux of metabolism and, in part, in stored energy in potential differences. If this assumption is true, it follows, then, that by studying potential differences during rest and during activity a record could be made of a general level of immediately available energy, as represented by algebraicly-summated boundary potentials.

In the face of the demand for activity this reservoir of potential energy could be tapped. When the biological system is at rest, the potentials could be recorded as DC potentials, but when protoplasm is thrown into any kind of activity, such as neural transmission, muscle contraction and similar events, the first sign of that activity would lie in the sudden withdrawal from the reservoir of electrical energy. In other words, a drop in potential differences. Then, mobilization of chemical properties might be expected to re-establish the original level of the potential difference.

Through studies of both DC and AC phenomena in the living system, it should be possible, therefore, to obtain straightforward records of fundamental biological activity. Since in a complex animal organization this is exceedingly difficult, not much progress has been made. In plants, which presumably are much simpler, the problem can be attacked more readily. For this reason, therefore, the studies of the electrical response associated with a stimulus to the sensitive plant, Mimosa, were made.

The most striking thing about the results is the very great similarity between the electrical response of the stimulus reaction in Mimosa to the electrical records of propagated electrical response of the action current in vertebrate neurones. The magnitude of the response is, of course, very much greater, and the time scale in seconds rather than in milliseconds.

Several seconds after a stimulus, whether a burn, a cutting or crushing, or a shock from a 90 volt B battery, a wave of increasing negativity appears under the hot or peripheral electrode. This peak arises to sixty or seventy millivolts and then subsides to the original voltage gradient and, though not always, often crosses it. This record is very similar to that of the spike in the neural action current. This spike lasts, however, from two to three seconds to five or six seconds. In younger, more active plants, the duration of the spike is apparently shorter than in the older ones. Following the spike, there is a positive after-potential followed by an upward swing of the potential difference which establishes a new level of negativity, lasting from a few minutes to several hours.

The whole wave form of this stimulus response is strikingly like the wave form of a single axone response in the vertebrate nervous system. Although the polarities differ, in all probability this is caused by a difference in the geometry of the electrode placement. Attempts were made to relate this to the anatomy of Mimosa, as it is well known in animals that the rate of conductivity of a nervous impulse is a function of the diameter of the axone. In Mimosa there are continuous fluid-containing channels which, conceivably, might be likened to a nerve process. These channels, however, are buried beneath the surface since they are covered by many layers of cells. The electrodes, of course, are in contact with the surface cells, not with the conducting channels. The whole system, however, is obviously conductive of electricity and it may be that the records obtained are derived from the longitudinal channels.

In Mimosa, the longitudinal channels vary in size, have thick walls, and are arranged in quadrants. They are centrally situated and covered by many layers of cells. In the rachis, the channels are more deeply placed peripherally and tend to scatter towards the circumference as the stem is approached. There does not seem to be any marked change in the size of the canals. In the stem the number of conductive systems increases markedly with a concomitant enlargement. Also, they lie nearer the surface and there are fewer layers of cells covering them. The difference in size of the channels may bear some significant relation to the electrical records if it should appear that the conducting canals are involved in the propagation of the stimulus.

The study here reported suggests that with Mimosa—as in the nervous system of animals—the rate of conduction of impulse is a function of the diameter of the channel. But this particular aspect of the problem needs to be investigated further.

If the recorded standing-potential represents the measure of a reservoir of electrical energy available for activity, then a stimulus such as that applied in Mimosa brings about a sudden withdrawal from that storehouse. The fact that a certain potential gradient with the periphery positive to the central region is necessary for the reaction, implies that unless the amount of electrical energy stored is at a designated level, the reaction cannot go forward. If, however, the level is high enough, the stimulus unlocks the storehouse and a wave of activity is propagated with a characteristic electrical correlate. It will be recalled that these experiments with Mimosa led a distinguished East Indian zoologist and philosopher to hold that such plants as Mimosa and, by inference, all other plants, possess a soul, exemplified in particular by the reaction of the system to an external stimulus!

The interesting thing about all these results to date makes it clear that the electrical properties of a living system are directly to be correlated with the genetic constitution of a living system, on the one hand, and on the other hand are modified by changes in the physical or chemical. The alteration, however, is not in pattern but in the magnitude of the typical response. This does not mean that there is a profound change in the electrical field, but only that the electrical field can be modified by an appropriate stimulus.

7

We had started our voyage of discovery by examining the most complex electro-dynamic fields—those of the human organism. We had also found fields in simpler forms of life—animals, eggs, seeds and plants. So it seemed desirable to extend our hunt for fields to the simplest living organization, protoplasm.

This was important, not only to make sure that everything that is alive possesses a field but also because protoplasm is the basic, formative material of animal forms. Whatever may trigger, too, the nervous system, a basic requirement is the energy made available by the incredibly-complex chemical flux of protoplasm.

The more, then, that we can discover about the elementary

properties of protoplasm, the better we will be able to understand how the nervous system functions.

Again, at the suggestion of Professor Sinnott, an examination was made of the electrical properties of a very simple protoplasmic system, that of the slime mould, Physarum polycephalum. This is a common mould which grows readily in the laboratory and exhibits characteristic patterns of growth and of fruiting. Also, its protoplasm is in constant movement, oscillating from one end of the system to the other. This streaming of protoplasm, of course, is well known to botanists, and offers many opportunities for investigation. The mould is a syncytium of protoplasm with no cell boundaries but many included nuclei. Since the material grows readily in quite adequate quantities, it makes an ideal elementary protoplasmic system for a further study of the electro-metric properties.

There were three primary objectives of this study: The first was to determine whether or not, in the living plasmodium, in constant movement, there exists an electrical correlate of this movement. Secondly, after the results of the Mimosa experiment, it was interesting to examine the possibility of an electro-metric response in the protoplasm to a variety of external stimuli, both chemical and physical. Finally, a third possibility was to examine the changes which might be found in the plasmodium when an external field was applied to it. There is plenty of evidence in the literature to show that changes in the electrical environment of protoplasm do produce observable effects on the protoplasm itself.

Using silver-silver chloride electrodes, a high input impedance amplifier and a recording galvanometer, many records were taken of the changing potential in a strand, or vein, of the plasmodium during the movement of the protoplasmic system itself. In the laboratory, using moving picture records and electro-metrics, the pulsating character of the growth of the slime mould was studied.

Under the microscope, it is simple to demonstrate that every sixty or ninety seconds the protoplasm in the veins reverses the direction of flow. The electrical pickup from the vein, combined with the moving picture, reveals that in the majority of instances polar reversal of the voltage occurs *before* there is a directional change of the plasmic flow, but also there are many instances where the change in both phenomena seem to occur simultaneously. This, undoubtedly, needs further study.

It is highly important, of course, to determine whether or not the change in potential is the result of the protoplasmic flow or the reverse of this. There is no evidence in the literature as to the nature of the forces which bring about this change in protoplasmic flow. Undoubtedly, this is involved in the growth of the whole system and is concerned, apparently, in part, with the search of the plasmodium for energy sources or food.

The rate at which the protoplasm moves undoubtedly is a function, to some extent, of temperatures in the environment. Although there are no exact records of these relationships, the fact remains that lowering the temperature does tend to slow up the flow of protoplasm. Certain conditions make it possible, moreover, to seek any electrical changes at times when the protoplasm is not flowing; and there have been records made in the laboratory which show that an electrical change in polarity in the plasmodium vein may occur in the absence of visible protoplasmic movement. There has not yet been observed, however, any lack of electrical correlates when protoplasm itself is moving.

That changes in the electrical environment have an effect upon the electrical properties of protoplasm, is well known from the studies of Lund and his associates, and more recently by Anderson. In this laboratory, Anderson's experiments were repeated, using the technique we have employed in our search for more information, and show that the reversal of polarity in the mould, by changing the external electrical environment, markedly inhibits the spread of the plasmodium. The direction in which the plasmodium grows, moreover, can be altered by, again, imposing an external electrical field on the primitive protoplasm. In every instance, the growing plasmodium could be made to turn towards the negative side of an imposed electrical environment. In other words, in the slime mould, changing the electrical environment can, under certain conditions, modify the direction in which energy flows in the protoplasmic system.

The third question—what is the electrical correlate of an adequate stimulus to the plasmodium—was studied using a cathode-ray tube as recording instrument, with photographic reproduction. Here, again, it was demonstrated that any change in the physical environment of primitive protoplasm results in an adequate stimulus to the protoplasm itself. For a single vein of the slime mould, suspended between two silver-silver chloride electrodes, showed a remarkable electro-metric response to such a stimulus as a tap on one of the electrodes.

Unlike the nervous system, however, there seemed to be a fairly close correlation between the strength of the tap and the electro-metric response of the protoplasm. A weak tap produced a relatively small change in voltage gradient, whereas a heavier one increased the magnitude of the electrical response. There was, however, obviously, a plateau of the response beyond which the protoplasm showed no further increase in voltage output. This, of course, is unlike the all-or-none phenomena to be found in neural protoplasm.

Records of this sort reinforce the concept that one of the simpler forms of protoplasm exhibits properties very like that to be found in the nervous system. This might be suspected, of course, since both neurones and the slime mould are built of the same basic stuff, protoplasm. Even the most primitive protoplasm, in order to maintain its existence, must be capable of responding to the changing physical and chemical environment, of transmitting the stimuli throughout its extent and after some kind of correlation or coordinating or integration of all the stimuli, of producing some kind of describable response. These basic properties of protoplasm, after all, are to be found enhanced enormously, specialized and increased in efficiency through the differentiation of the nervous system.

No less important are changes in the chemical environment. For example, if a drop of 2% procain is placed on a vein, the immediate effect of the application of the drop—and this is true also of water—is a stimulus response usually in the opposite polarity to the tap stimulus. After a matter of a few minutes, however, the tap will produce a much reduced and flattened response; the magnitude is lessened and a return to the baseline is slow.

If the procain is washed off with a fine spray of tap water, within another five minutes a reasonably characteristic response

78

is obtained, but much enhanced over the pre-test situation. It should be noted that the vein hangs suspended in the air over a moist chamber and the procain can be either adsorbed to the surface of the protoplasm or pass through the phase boundary into the protoplasm itself. The promptness of the recovery act of washing and the enhancement of the response would seem to indicate that the adsorbtion to the surface was the more probable.

These experiments suggest that slime mould could become a very valuable tool for the study of the effect of changing chemical environment on protoplasm. In general, the similarity in electrical response of the slime mould to changes in the physical and chemical environment shows a remarkable similarity to the properties of neural tissue.

*   *   *

With the experiments described in this chapter we had covered a wide range of living forms and in all of them we had found electro-dynamic fields. But our adventure was to lead us to still further discoveries.

CHAPTER FIVE

The Field as a Signpost

1

We had reason to believe that the electro-dynamic field could serve as a signpost for a variety of conditions because our experiments had confirmed our basic assumption. This was that the organism possesses a field as a whole which embraces subsidiary or local fields, representing the organism's component parts. We assumed, then, that variations in the subsidiary fields would be reflected in variations in the flow of energy in the whole system—as we had found in ovulation and malignancy. We decided, therefore, to look for further practical consequences of the theory.

Working with Dr. Samuel Harvey and Dr. Max Taffel, of the Yale University School of Medicine, we initiated a study of the relationship between the electro-metrics of the peripheral nervous system and the physiological state of the system examined. With the cooperation of Dr. R. G. Grennel, we made a special study of so-called surface potentials and peripheral nerve injury.

In the course of these experiments, it was demonstrated that—in experimental animals and man—surface potential differences do reflect peripheral nerve activities. These potentials are not affected by pre-ganglionic sympathectomy and seem to be independent of vascular and sweating responses.

We soon found a definite relationship between nerve and tissue in the form of a potential difference, which can be used in quantitative tests of nerve function. These tests are simple enough for routine clinical application. They show a clear-cut correlation between the integrity of the peripheral somatic nervous system and potential differences measured on the surface.

Interference, pharmacological or traumatic, with normal functions of ulnar or sciatic nerve is reflected in an altered standing potential between a reference electrode and a moving electrode in contact with the area supplied by the nerve in question. The mechanism by which this correlation is brought about is important. Complicity of the vascular bed might exist but the lack of any significant change in the pattern following sympathectomy makes this unlikely. However, the sympathectomies were all pre-ganglionic and hence further work must be done in order to clarify the matter.

It has been found that rapidly shutting off the blood-flow in the forearm and hand by means of a blood pressure cuff on the arm, as well as a sudden return of flow on releasing the cup, does not significantly alter the potential difference. In other words, altering the normal functioning of the vascular bed does not affect the standing potential.

Furthermore, since the microvoltmeter is relatively unaffected by changes in resistance in the system being measured, 'skin resistance' and sweating, as reported by Richter and his associates, are not involved in the potential changes. In the light of these findings it would seem unlikely that the sympathetic nervous system is the mediating factor. Nevertheless, the data show that in unilateral sympathectomy there is a difference in the standing potential on the operated and unoperated sides. These measurements, then, form the basis of a simple, quantitative test of peripheral function, independent of sweating or of vascular reaction.

These ventures into the unknown of the electro-metrics of living organisms were often prompted by a search for answers to practical questions. An example of this are the electro-metrics of wound healing.

The late Dr. Samuel Harvey and Dr. Max Taffel had been studying wound healing in experimental animals and in man; and had called attention to the fact that the strength of a healing wound is probably caused in large measure by proliferations of fibroblast. This means, of course, that there is a great deal of mitotic activity going on and, since an increase in the number of cells is a vital biological property—and since other experiments to be reported later show a close correlation with growth—these studies by Taffel and Harvey showed an increase in tensile strength correlated with the passage of time.

This increase varies, for the most part, during the first eight or ten days following the incision. This tends to be modified in vitamin C deficient animals. But the increase of tensile strength must involve at least two processes: one of cell proliferation and one of cell differentiation. In normal development, the two events do not occur in the same cell simultaneously. Each cell takes part in the generalized mitosis of a group of cells—probably fibroblasts—for a period of time, after which, with other cells, it undergoes a period of differentiation. As growth proceeds, new cells go into mitosis and then into differentiation adding thereby to the new structure. There are no known methods for differentiating these two processes except by microscopic examination. The electro-metric technique offers the possibility of discriminating between the two.

2

It seemed advisable, therefore, to investigate the nature of bioelectric phenomena in wound healing and to discover any possible relationship between bioelectrics and tensile strength and also between bioelectrics and growth or differentiation.

The experimental animals used for the laboratory were guinea pigs, one group of which were fed a controlled diet. Another group were fed a form of laboratory diet. In both sets of studies an area of skin was bared and measurements taken between the cephalic end of the bare area, and another at the caudal end of the area. Wherever incision was to be made between the two, a control point was taken.

After the preliminary measurements were made, the skin and subcutaneous fascia were incised and sutured, following which another set of examinations were made. These were continued daily for the next two weeks or until the wound was healed. In some instances, the healing was so complete as to make it difficult to determine the site of the wound.

The data showed a marked change of potential gradient between the normal skin and the area of injury. Perhaps the most astonishing finding was that the site of injury was not consistently negative to the normal tissue, as would be expected by the theory of injury potential. On the contrary, for the first twenty-four or twenty-eight hours after the injury, the wound area was positive to the cephalic point in the normal skin. The potential gradient between these two points tended to rise for twenty-four or twenty-eight hours and then rapidly to decline until the third or fourth day when the wound became negative to the normal skin. This negativity increased until the maximum was reached on the eighth or ninth day. Following this, and lasting for twenty-four to forty-eight hours, the potential gradient dropped, to be followed on the tenth or twelfth day by another rise in potential. This was repeated on the twelfth and fourteenth day. On the fifteenth or sixteenth day the gradients returned to approximately normal limits.

The comparison of the curves obtained by Harvey and Taffel shows an interesting parallelism. The tensile strength measurements show a rapidly rising curve during the first eight days. The bioelectric measurements show a similar change. After the eighth day, the tensile strength seems to approach a plateau. The bioelectric determinations show alternating growth and differentiation after the eighth day. While examinations show rather slow changes in the potential gradients, nevertheless, they are statistically reliable.

In order to investigate this matter further, a second series of animals was studied under somewhat different conditions. Thirty guinea pigs from the laboratory stock were taken, ten of which were placed on a controlled laboratory diet. It is to be noted that this diet was different from that of the first series. These animals received an incision on the right flank as described, and were read daily.

The rise and fall of potential differences during this period would seem to be correlated with the growth of fibroblasts. Then followed a period of differentiation represented by a clear-cut increase in potential differences.

However, once started, the alternation of growth and differentiation was strikingly parallel in both groups of animals. Twenty of the animals were put on a vitamin C deficient diet— ten with no wounds in the skin and ten with wounds. The potential gradients in the operated and unoperated scorbutic animals, and in the normals on a controlled diet, showed interesting parallelisms.

In the case of unoperated scorbutics a reasonably constant baseline appeared through the period of the experiment. The operated scorbutics, however, showed changes in the potential differences which closely paralleled the normal animals, save that the magnitude of the potential difference was less. In addition, they showed the same delay in the onset of potential rise as was seen in the operated animals on the normal diet. These observations indicated that it is possible to measure with some certainty bioelectric concomitants of growth and differentiation in the healing of wounds in the guinea pig. They suggested that the growth process is not a continuous one, except in the early stages, but rather that, after the eighth day, it alternates with periods of differentiation. Bioelectric correlates of growth in the animals on a control diet seem to rise faster and reach a greater magnitude than in the case of the scorbutic animals.

3

In cooperation with the above-mentioned surgeons, a further experiment was made on wound healing in the human. Some twenty-five instances of operative procedures, with uncomplicated healing of the wounds, were selected for study. All these healed without any evidence of infection. Determinations of the potential gradient between two points—one in the immediate vicinity of the wound, and another at some distance from it— were made daily, beginning on the day following the operation and continuing until the patient was discharged from the hospital, usually after fourteen days. In each observation, sufficient readings were taken to insure valid measurements.

It was at once apparent that there was, on the whole, a definite trend. Comparison of individual cases revealed in many instances wide discrepancies. Such variations have been found to be consistently present in animals studied by the tensile strength method. Similar variations were particularly characteristic of electro-metric technique and therefore many determinations are necessary.

The results show that there is a phase of positive potential of some four days' duration corresponding to the so-called lag in the tensile strength method. This same phenomenon was observed in the guinea pigs and also in mice as an accompaniment of a carcinogenic irritation. Following this, the wound passes into a proliferated phase during which a negative potential is encountered which reaches its height between the seventh and ninth days. Here the maximum negative voltage is reached at approximately the same time as the maximum tensile strength. The increasing negativity suggests an homology with the rising negativity observed in other animals and in cancer.

At the end of the tenth day the wound is usually healed and from then to the end of the determinations the voltage gradients gradually fall to the normal base-line. These observations of electro-metric studies of the healing wound in man parallel those made in experimental animals and give weight to the concept that the process of healing in man is a phenomenon of growth.

4

Since these wound healing experiments on man seem to indicate a modification of the normal picture after surgery, it behooved us to find out what went on from day to day in normal human beings with a reasonably normal existence. To this end, a group of ten medical students were found to agree to do the necessary examination to see what happened in the ordinary day-to-day existence of such apparently normal subjects.

These were studied for a considerable period of time and it was found, in general, that the students could be separated into three groups as was mentioned in Chapter 3 : one, a group that showed consistently high potential differences between the index fingers of the two hands, another with a low potential difference, and a third, an intermediate point.

There was, however, one particular student in the group who consistently showed a higher potential difference than all the rest of the subjects. On investigation, it was found that this boy had a history of emotional instability and, at the time he was admitted, was admitted as an experiment. Before the end of the year, however, the boy became definitely psychotic and had to be remanded to an institution.

These findings suggested at once that deviations from a normal behaviour, such as might appear in a psychotic, were worth investigating further. With the cooperation of the late Dr. Eugen Kahn in the Department of Psychiatry, a number of patients—who had been studied carefully by the psychiatric staff—were selected and measurements made on them daily for a considerable period of time.

The psychiatrists were asked to divide the patients into three groups—obvious deviates from normal behaviour, those that were reasonably normal, and an intermediate group. The electro-metric experiments were carried out in the services of the psychiatric hospital without the electro-metric investigator knowing anything about the status of the individual.

At the conclusion of the electro-metrics the patients were divided into three groups: those with markedly changed electro-metrics, those with relatively little change, and an intermediate group. Subsequently, the intermediate group was subdivided into a high-low group and a low-high group.

At the conclusion of the experiment, the groups selected by the psychiatrists were compared with the groups selected by the electro-metric investigator, who—it should be emphasized—knew nothing about the psychiatric diagnosis. *Results of the study showed clearly enough that the group consisting of those markedly deviated from normal behaviour by psychiatric examination also showed a similar deviation in electro-metric examination.*

The low group, likewise, paralleled each other perfectly. But in the intermediate group, as might be expected, there was considerable variation in both the psychiatric reports and in the electro-metric readings. This, of course, is very interesting and it

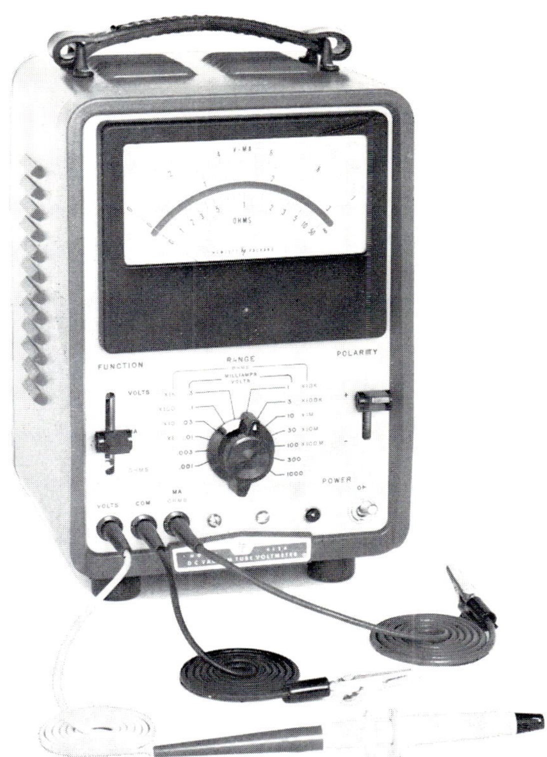

Specifications of Hewlett-Packard D.C. Vacuum Tube Voltmeter Model 412A recommended by Dr Burr to measure electrodynamic fields.

Voltmeter

...age Range: Positive and negative voltages from 1 volt full scale to 1,000 volts full scale in thirteen ...es.

...uracy: ±1% of full scale on any range.

...t Resistance:
...egohms ±1% on 1 mV, 3 mV, and 10 mV ranges.
...egohms ±1% on 30 mV range.
...megohms ±1% on 100 mV range.
...megohms ±1% on 300 mV range and above.

...Rejection: A voltage at power line or twice power frequency 40 dB greater than full scale affects reading ...than 1%. Peak voltage must not exceed 1,500 volts.

...ages and Currents:

...e	Open Circuit Volts	Short Circuit Current
	10 mV	10 mA
	100 mV	10 mA
...	1 V	10 mA
...0	1 V	1 mA
...K	1 V	100 µA
...0K	1 V	10 µA
	1 V	1 µA
...M	1 V	0·1 µA
...0M	1 V	0·01 µA

...o courtesy Hewlett-Packard
...Alto, California and Slough, Bucks.

General

Meter: Individually calibrated.

Isolation Resistance: At least 100 megohms shunted by 0·01 µF between common terminal and case (power line) ground.

Isolation: May be operated up to 500 V dc or 130 V ac from ground.

Power: 115 or 230 volts ± 10%, 50 to 60 Hz, 35 watts.

Dimensions:

Cabinet Mount: 11½″ high, 7½″ wide, 10″ deep. (292 × 191 × 254 mm).

Weight:

Cabinet Mount: Net, 12 lbs. (5·5 kg). Shipping, 14 lbs. (6·4 kg).

Rack Mount: Net, 12 lbs. (5·5 kg.) Shipping, 20 lbs. (9·0 kg).

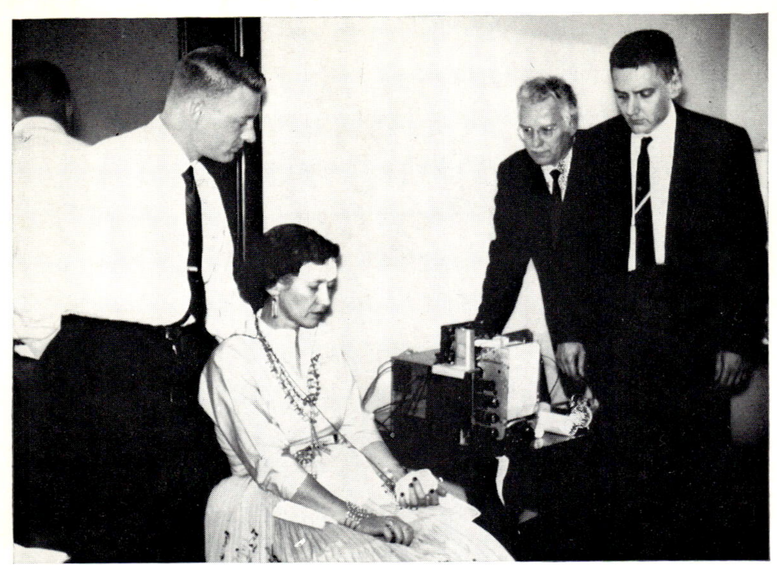

First public demonstration of subject going into trance connected to volt meter.

Photo-electric tracing showing various stages of hypnosis and post-hypnotic emotion.

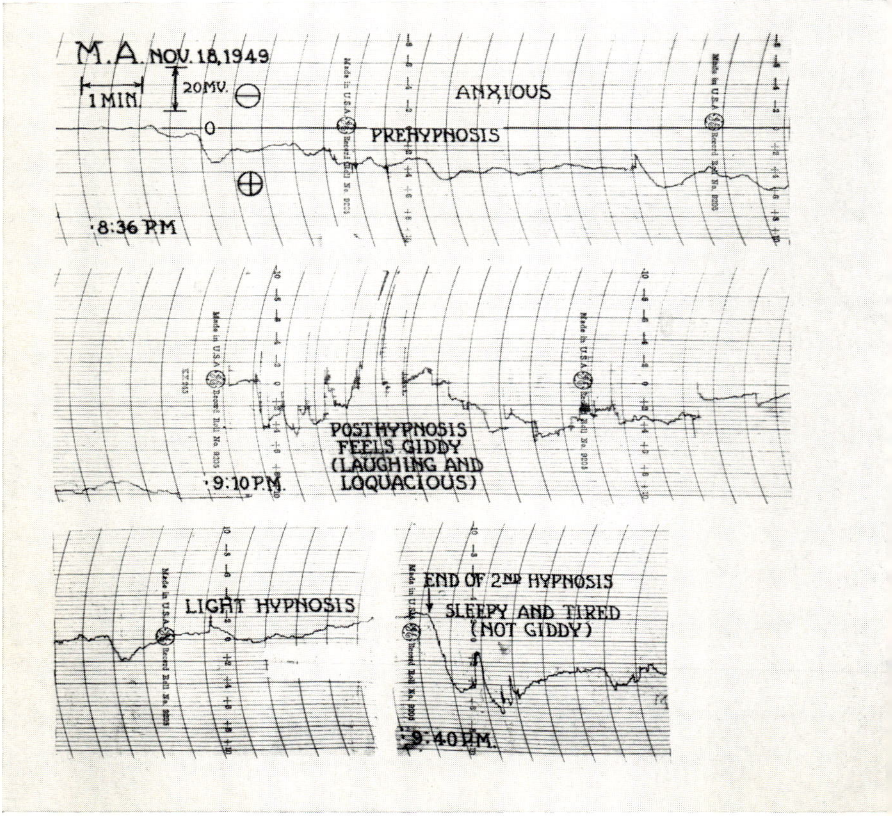

suggested that the electro-metric technique might be useful in the neurological and psychiatric fields.

This whole area has been extensively investigated by Dr. Leonard J. Ravitz, Jr. at one time on the staff of the Department of Psychiatry at Yale, and followed by him through appointments in a number of other institutions. His results are striking and extraordinary. Perhaps the most remarkable result obtained in our laboratory by Dr. Ravitz was when he found a significant electro-metric correlate of hypnotism that was astonishing to watch: *a continuously-recording voltmeter showed evidence of marked changes in voltage gradient during the hypnotic process.*

This was not an event which might be related to the subjectivity of the operator, but could be recorded without argument on the recording galvanometer. If anyone needed objective evidence of the results of hypnosis, one needed only to look at the charts recorded under these conditions. Needless to say, this suggests an enormous range of studies which could be made paralleling those of Dr. Ravitz and, wherever possible, extending them.

It becomes evident from Dr. Ravitz's examination that by using electro-metric techniques on patients in psychiatric hospitals, patients—as a result of therapy, or changing circumstances—could safely be discharged from the hospital when the voltage gradient indicated a reasonable return to normal. Likewise, electro-metrics could show clearly enough when certain patients—no matter what the therapy was—could *not* be returned safely to normal life outside of the institution. The value of this to the institutionalized psychotic should be apparent at once.

Needless to say, a great deal more study is needed and much more data must be collected. But Dr. Ravitz's striking results are exciting enough to warrant the expenditure of the additional time and effort to extend these studies further.

Such studies are all the more desirable because—as mentioned in Chapter 1—L-field measurements can serve as signposts to emotional instability outside institutions and could therefore serve as a valuable tool to the Armed Forces and to industry.

Practical applications apart, there are also great psychological and philosophical implications in the discovery that the state of the mind is reflected in the state of the field. Another remarkable experiment by Dr. Ravitz, too, in which an emotion of grief recalled under hypnotic regression caused a 14-millivolt rise for two-and-a-half minutes, suggests other possibilities. Already field measurements can point to emotional conditions; in the future they may also be used as a purely objective, quantitative assessment of emotion.

It cannot be too strongly emphasized that the electro-metric approach to emotional diagnosis can be completely impersonal and objective. The electro-metric investigator of psychiatric patients mentioned a short while ago did not know—and did not need to know—the mental state of the patients. Yet his electro-metric findings tallied closely with the psychiatric diagnoses.

Since the electro-metric tests are simple and since any competent technician can quickly be trained to make them, in many cases they can be used to save the time of busy psychiatrists by sorting out all but the borderline cases. This can not only save time but also a great deal of expense to the patient or taxpayer.

5

In this age, probably more people are subjected to emotional stress—from environmental or other causes—than in any previous one. Our bulging mental hospitals are sufficient evidence of this; and, outside our mental hospitals, more and more people seem to feel the need for psychiatric help.

Modern psychosomatic medicine has demonstrated that, unfortunately, the effects of emotional disturbance are often not confined to mental symptoms: many physical ills have a psychosomatic origin.

Faced with this vast problem, we have to admit a distressing lack of knowledge not only of the true nature of mind or emotion but also of the mechanism of the relationship between mind and body.

L-field measurements, of course, cannot solve this problem. But, it is submitted, they can offer some new approaches to its solution. They can give early warning of emotional instability—as we have seen—and one day, perhaps, will offer a reliable means

88

of measuring its intensity.

This could be useful not only to psychiatrists and psychologists but also to practitioners of internal medicine. With the intense modern pressures on the medical profession, the average doctor simply does not have the time to elicit the emotional pressures which—he may suspect—are the real cause of his patient's physical problems, especially as many patients are reluctant to disclose them. If, however, electro-metric tests could quickly reveal the *existence* of these pressures—they cannot, of course, disclose their *nature*—they could be of material help to the doctor in devising the best treatment for his patient.

As we noted in Chapter 1, regular electro-metric tests of healthy men and women could help them to avoid or to handle dangerous situations. They could also help less emotionally-stable people to avoid—at their 'low' periods—situations which might subject them to intolerable emotional stress.

The relationship between the state of the electro-dynamic field and abnormal physical conditions—of which the experiments described in the preceding pages afford abundant evidence—suggests the 'mechanism' of psychosomatic illness. For, since the state of the mind is reflected in the state of the field, it is not too hard to imagine *how* business worries or an unhappy marriage can produce ulcers.

Last—but not least—the discovery that the state of the mind can affect the state of the field should induce a new sympathy for the emotionally distressed. We should no longer be so ready to brush off their miseries with the remark: 'it's all in their imagination.' Perhaps it is. But if an emotion—even one recalled by hypnosis—is able to affect a voltmeter it cannot be lightly dismissed as a figment, whatever its origin. It has a definite reality. As Dr. Ravitz has put it:

'Both emotional activity and stimuli of any sort involve mobilization of electric energy, as indicated on the galvanometer. Hence, both emotions and stimuli evoke the same energy. Emotions can be equated with energy.'

6

Behaviour is the reaction of a living system to the co-ordinated and integrated stimuli resulting from changes in the physical and chemical environments. In the case of man, at least, to the physical factors of environment the ideological environment must also be added because an idea is just as valid a stimulus to the nervous system as a kick in the teeth.

As a matter of fact, it can be shown, without much question, that ideas are actually more important as stimuli to the nervous system than any of the others. One needs only to look at the history of the outstanding figures of the last two or three hundred years who, rightly or wrongly, had ideas which profoundly affected whole generations. This is true of dictators, politicians, philosophers, religionists or military leaders.

As ideas are—or induce—emotions which evoke energy in the nervous system, electro-metric studies of this phenomenon seem relevant to the study of human behaviour, even if they offer no hope of improving it. At the least we may be able to learn a little about how the machine works, even if we cannot understand how the driving ideas originate.

Though man, over the years, has acquired an extraordinary control over his physical environment, the problem of human relations remains unsolved. We seem to be no better off in dealing with each other than were our remote ancestors. Part of the reason for this, of course, is to be found in the enormous complexity of the nervous system of man and the lack of real understanding of the way the protoplasm of nervous tissue operates. So any approach to the problem of human behaviour should start with a better understanding of the nervous system. For whether it is an idea, an emotion or a kick in the teeth which triggers the activity of the nervous system, a basic requirement, needless to say, is the storehouse of energy made available by the chemical flux of protoplasm as noted in the previous chapter.

Though the energy required to make an adjustment is derived from this chemical activity, the direction in which the energy flows, and the way in which it is used, is a consequence of the pattern of organization of neural tissues. It is not enough, therefore, to know the details of the complex structures involved, but rather to have some over-all grasp and understanding of the way the nervous system works. Analysis of the units is of vital importance, even down to the sub-microscopic level, but equally important is a grasp of the relationships between all the component parts.

Since behaviour, moreover, is the result, in part, of the impact of one organism on another, no real picture of the forces which make man operate the way he does is possible without a complete knowledge and understanding of the structure and function of the nervous system.

The results of many years of study have tended to emphasize certain rather stereotyped activities. As a result, the electrical circuit analogies tended to lead investigators away from the basic fact that each neurone is in itself a living organism. These electrical circuit analogies, partly inspired by the modern computer, are derivable directly from the fundamental property of protoplasm, and more particularly, from the all-or-none response of a nerve cell.

Even the simplest protoplasmic system can be stimulated by changes in the physical, chemical and ideological environment, can transmit these effects through its substance, can coordinate, correlate and integrate all the varieties of stimuli and can, as a result, make that adjustment necessary for the continued existence of the system. The behaviour of even the simplest organism is parodic in that it 'functions in accordance with its inherent design'.* One of the greatest difficulties in assaying behaviour lies in its complexity, in the lack of objective measurement and in a very great influence of the subjective.

In the literature, the description of behaviour of even the simplest organisms is coloured by anthropomorphisms. The critical study of behaviour, moreover, almost invariably involves some disturbance in the organism under study. Ideally, any measurement must involve no alteration in the thing measured during the measurement. This is difficult to achieve even in

* King, 1945.

physical systems. It is peculiarly difficult in biological systems unless we employ the techniques described in the preceding pages.

Our experiments had offered some signposts to a better understanding of the human nervous system. We had found with corn kernels—it will be remembered—evidence of a close correlation between a measurable, electro-metric characteristic and both the genetic constitutions and also their subsequent productivity in the field.

A study, too, of the sensitive plant Mimosa, had yielded evidence that in this particular living form, the protoplasmic mechanism showed characteristics very similar to those found in the nervous system. In other words, the nervous system in higher forms and in a relatively-simple system like a plant had similar electro-metric responses.

All this, admittedly, is a very modest approach to a better understanding of the human nervous system. But, at least, it is a beginning and, as Confucius said: 'The longest journey starts with the first step.'

Perhaps the most important aspect of the first step is that L-field measurements make it possible to *measure* the effects of various stimuli to the nervous system. For, in the history of science, the ability to measure something has often—if not always—been the foundation-stone of progress.

7

As everyone knows, there is speculation whether the Universe is an expanding one or a closed system, whether it is governed by a static set of laws or is a dynamic, active Universe in which growth and development occur. It is clear enough that the laws of the Universe, as we know them, are not happenstance phenomena but are closely integrated in a unit.

The statement that the biologist makes, that the living organism is more than the sum of its parts, applies equally to the Universe. The living organism, also, is a whole unit, no part of which can go off on a tangent by itself without disaster to the living system. There is no reason to suppose that this same general principle cannot be applied to human behaviour, for human behaviour is not the result of the imposition of legalistic and moral laws on the biological laws of the organism, but rather behaviour is the conseqence of the activity of the nervous system of man. The nervous system of man is an organized, designed, dynamic machine.

Many people object at once to this spuriously-labelled 'materialistic' approach to the Universe. But this is nonsense. The Universe is not only a machine but also has certain qualitative attributes. We talk about the beauty of the star-filled night, the odour of a bed of lilies-of-the-valley; and we could go on almost indefinitely listing the qualitative attributes of the things that are common to our environment.

These qualitative characteristics do not control the physical system but are attributes of it, and if our modern concepts are anywhere near right, there is an interchange, which the experts call 'feed-back relationships', between the qualitative attributes of the physical system and the activity of the system itself. Just how this is accomplished, we do not know. We ought to know, and in time we probably will know.

In the meantime, we should remember the fact—pointed out by Sir Charles Sherrington several decades ago—that the mind of man does not exist in time, does not occupy space, and involves, so far as anyone knows, no energy transformations. But the nervous system, through which the mind of man works, does exist in time, does occupy space, and does require energy transformations.

Admittedly, this is a mystery. How can a non-material attribute such as the mind of man actually influence the organic nervous system? It can be argued that moral law is an example of this kind of thing. Moral or spiritual laws do not exist in time, do not occupy space and, so far as anyone knows, do not involve energy transformations, and yet we have evidence, sketchy to be sure, that the so-called spiritual side of existence, does influence human behaviour. How this discrepancy between mind and body achieves this, no one knows.

There is one profound difference, however, between natural and moral laws. Moral laws are not laws operative in the Universe—the laws of Nature—but are sheer inventions of the mind of man. Man, unfortunately, is an egocentric person. He is primarily concerned with himself, his continued existence and his sense of well-being as he adjusts to his physical and mental environment. Everything he does, therefore, tends to be coloured by his own personal stake in the matter.

No one of us has any personal stake in the law of gravitation; we know it operates and we know we cannot get along without it, unless we substitute other kinds of forces to counteract it. It is a fundamental property of things. But there is nothing in any of the spiritual or moral laws which has the same characteristic. It behooves us to get on the ball and discover what we can, so that a spiritual law which is good in New York and Boston and Washington, is equally good in Hongkong, Bangkok and Timbuktu. Only when we can find the fundamental properties of the spiritual or moral law and, for that matter, of the legal laws, can we hope to find any kind of satisfactory answer to the problem of mankind.

The problem of human behaviour is still the greatest problem that faces mankind. We have not solved it. As a matter of fact we are really making no attempt to solve it. To be sure, many dedicated people are endeavouring to find out the details of how the nervous system works, in the hope that this will give some clues as to how we can integrate and co-ordinate our human attitudes to each other and to the Universe. Up to date, however, the results have not been particularly fruitful.

What we need to do is to apply the methods of science to the problem of human interrelationships. The methods of science have been deified in recent years because of the remarkable advances which have resulted from their application to the study of the physical universe.

As we mentioned in the first chapter the method of science involves first of all a reasonable contact with the background of the particular subject we are investigating, its natural history. Out of this someone comes along with a creative mind and sees unsuspected relationships in this background. This gives rise to a hunch, a theory, an assumption. In physics and chemistry the logical consequences of this assumption are then put to laboratory tests and if, in the laboratory, the results tend to confirm the assumption, we generally believe that our theory is correct. This, of course, is not necessarily so because there might be other assumptions for which this same data will be a valid result.

When it comes to applying this method to humans, we are faced with the very real problem that control of the experimental set-up of mankind is far from easy. We have not been able to do it, but some day, someone with a creative mind will make it possible for us to begin to use and apply the methods of science to this problem. If we can do this, we probably can arrive at some significant additions to its solution.

In the last analysis, the Universe is a unit, all of its parts are related to the wholeness of the Universe, and there is necessarily some interrelationship between the wholeness of the Universe and the activities of its individual components. From the unified theory of Einstein—even though it lacked final, complete validation with respect to the law of gravity—it is clear that one of the characteristics of the Universe are fields which can be measured by instruments. It does not make any difference whether you call it an electro-static field, an electro-magnetic field, or an electro-dynamic field. The name is always a consequence of the methods which were applied to its study. In other words, there is one unifying characteristic of the Universe which we have ignored, and that is its field properties. We should see, therefore, if we can find some significant characteristics of the field properties of the Universe which can be put to use by mankind in this incredibly difficult problem of human relationships. There must be generalities in this field theory which can be discovered and which can be harnessed by mankind to help him solve his own problems.

The electro-dynamic fields which control the human organism are signposts to the most promising trail that future explorers can follow.

CHAPTER SIX

Antennae to the Universe

1

It was logical to deduce from the Field Theory that external electrical fields would affect the fields of living organisms. For, just as the overall L-field of the organism embraces and controls its subsidiary fields, the electrical environment of the earth includes —and can be expected to influence—the fields of the living forms on this planet.

This was something we could not easily check with human or animal subjects because each organism is not only unique but also constantly changing, as our experiments had shown. With the rapidly-fluctuating voltage-variations in humans and animals, it is extremely difficult to arrive at a steady baseline or norm from which to measure the influence of external forces, which are often slow in their cyclical variations.

It was most important, however, to try to detect the effects— if any—of external forces for three reasons. First, if we could demonstrate experimentally a logical deduction from the Field Theory, this would offer the Theory additional support. Second, if the electrical environment does affect the living organism, the more we could find out about those effects the better. Third, if we could establish that living forms are affected by their electrical environment, this would show that man is an integral part of the Universe and subject to the great forces that act across space, just as the earth itself is.

For these reasons we decided to carry out a long-term study of a living system which would be its own control, with the changes in internal and external factors to be supplied by Nature. Our aim was to examine, over a very long period of time, the electrical properties of the system and their relationship to environmental phenomena. The latter included, of course, temperature, humidity, barometric pressure, sunshine and dark and any other factors that we might be able to detect, measure and describe.

We chose a tree as the most suitable subject for this investigation because, in many ways, a tree has enormous advantages. It always stays put in a particular place; it requires no special feeding; it does not have to be anaesthetized when making the measurements; and there is no problem of cleaning up after the experiments, as there is with animals in the laboratory.

We hoped, then, that trees would not only offer a steady and reliable baseline from which to measure ordinary environmental influences but would also serve as antennae—so to speak—to pick up any extraterrestrial or Universal forces that might influence the living forms of this planet.

2

Since the pioneer studies of Lund, it has been known that trees exhibit electrical characteristics. So it was reasonable to expect that we could measure these over long periods of time if we could find a suitable way to place our electrodes permanently in contact with the cambium layer—the growing area of trees—with a 'bridge' of physiological salt solution to avoid any side-effects from the electrodes.

We anticipated no difficulty in measuring the potential gradients in the tree at any given time. But, if we were to detect environmental factors, we must prepare for the long haul and make sure that our electrodes and recording instruments would remain stable and reliable for many years.

If we could achieve this, we also hoped that our experiments with trees would answer another question: There seemed to be no doubt that the voltage gradients we had measured in living forms were the result of an unequal distribution of charged particles on either side of phase boundaries. This uneven distribution might be caused, of course, merely by the constantly-changing chemical flux of the protoplasm. But was this the sole explanation of the voltage gradients? Only a long-term study could settle this question.

If chemistry is the only factor in voltage gradients, one might expect wide variations in voltage gradients, both in magnitude and polarity as the chemistry of the organism changes from time to time. A tree is a highly-organized living system in an environment in which change is a constant factor and might therefore be expected to have other significant voltage variations.

Our first 'antenna to the Universe' was a young maple tree outside my house in New Haven, Connecticut, which could be connected to recording instruments in the house. At first glance this might seem a simple matter but, as we were trying something entirely new, it took a long time and many experiments before we developed a technique which proved satisfactory through several decades.

The bark of the tree was carefully removed down to the cambium layer and every effort was made to avoid injury to the layer itself because it is well known that injury-potentials in living organisms do occur. Fortunately, they do not last very long and if, unavoidably, we injured the cambium the effects would disappear in a short time.

After many months of careful experiment on a number of different kinds of trees we found that the best technique was to use small plastic containers with one open face, filled with physiological salt jelly in which the silver-silver chloride electrodes were embedded. The open face of the plastic container was held, under the bark, against the cambium layer.

It must again be emphasized that metallic electrodes in direct contact with protoplasm in living organisms set up unpredictable non-reproducible voltage gradients, which are caused by changes in the properties of the phase boundary between metal and protoplasm. As we have seen, however, if contact is made through a saline 'bridge' and with proper electrodes, reliable and reproducible voltage gradients can be recorded, with the aid of high input-impedance amplifiers.

After much experiment we found it best to place the containers holding the electrodes on the trunk of the tree, one above

98

the other, about three feet apart. The lower electrode was placed high enough on the tree trunk to avoid interference by marauding animals. The other electrode, three feet above, was reasonably safe from interference.

From the very beginning consistent, continuous and relatively-steady standing potentials were recorded. Preliminary experiments were begun in 1938 and almost continuous records were kept up to 1968.

Maple, elm and oak trees have been examined and it appears evident that the faster-growing trees, such as the maple, exhibit a somewhat higher potential than the slower-growing elm and a definitely higher potential than the still slower-growing oak.

As a double check, we established another 'antenna' in the form of an old, large elm tree outside my laboratory in the country, at Lyme, Connecticut. Simultaneously, too, we carried out similar experiments on an alligator pear in the laboratory.

With recording galvanometers drawing a trace of changing voltage gradients in all three sets of experiments, it was possible to determine to what extent a young maple tree in the city, an old elm in the country and an alligator pear in the laboratory might exhibit parallel changes.

3

It has long been known that there are diurnal rhythms in living systems. Recurrent events occur in living systems which provide a rhythm, or a cycle, which seems to be related partly to environmental circumstances and partly to others. There have been a number of explanations of these rhythms; and the general opinion seems to be that there are at least two factors involved. One, of course, is the actual metabolism of protoplasm. This, however, may or may not be a continuous source of energy. Much more likely it is an intermittent process.

On the other hand, it has been suggested that the changes in measurable characteristics of living systems are caused by hyperplasia, mitosis, or cell division. Mitosis goes on in the cambium of the tree and results in the changing diameter of the tree, as has been well established by numerous studies of trees under a variety of circumstances. The growing tips of trees also show mitosis, the result of which is a change in the length, for example, of parts of the plant system.

Therefore, in the tree at Lyme, instruments were provided not only to measure voltage gradients but also the changing diameter of the tree, all on a continuous basis. Tree-diameter was measured by a dendograph loaned by Professor Lutz of the Forestry School of Yale University.

The results, in the early stages of these experiments in measuring changing diameter and potential differences, were surprising. Recurrent events in the changing potential were obvious. During the hours from midnight to sunrise in the early morning, voltage gradients were relatively low but constant. With the beginning of daylight, a change occurred with a marked increase in the magnitude of the potential differences, usually reaching a height around noon. These changes were recorded over a three month period in the summers of 1943 and 1944.

A number of interesting results were apparent. During the early part of the summer and until September, there was a close relationship between the rise and fall of potential and the changing diameter of the tree. And at the time these records were made, this seemed like an extraordinary correlation between the growth of the cambium and the voltage gradient.

In September of 1943 and again in 1944, however, marked changes in voltage gradient of a recurrent character appeared but the diameter of the tree no longer changed.

This points up the fact that short-time studies of living systems are often misleading. The apparently-beautiful correlation between cambium growth and voltage gradient disappeared in a long-range study. This implied that the voltage gradient was not in itself the consequence of mitosis in the cambium of the tree. There must have been some other factor involved since it was clear enough that these changes showed no necessary causal dependency.

4

That there are changes in the electrical characteristics of the surround of the earth was shown long ago by the late Professor Harlan Stetson, of the Cosmic Ray Terrestrial Research Laboratory of the Massachusetts Institute of Technology. He drew attention to the fact that changes in the ionosphere significantly affect radio reception; and this phenomenon, of vital importance to the communication industries, has been studied extensively ever since.

It seemed worthwhile, therefore, to design an experiment in which continuous records of changing potential in a living system were made synchronously with careful records of changing temperature, humidity, barometric pressure, sun spots and Cosmic rays. For we thought that a comparison of these simultaneous records would enable us to determine whether any correlates between any of these variables existed.

With the aid of a grant from the National Institute of Health, a more elaborate experiment was devised to examine possible interrelationships with the electrical environment, to be continued over as long a period of time as possible. The experiment included four reasonably simultaneous records of changing voltage gradients in an Elm tree, a Maple tree, in the atmosphere adjacent, and in the earth.

Since we had many years of records of pure voltage differences in trees, there was available a valuable baseline of information about the changing electrical properties of a living system during the passage of time. As a result, we knew what to expect as a result of changing seasons, lunar cycles and diurnal rhythms. The two new records of variations in air and earth voltages could add to this information about the trees, and could offer clues as to the possible impact of the electrical environment on living processes.

The instrumentation included four high input-impedance amplifiers, two pairs of silver-silver chloride electrodes—a pair for each of two elms—an atmospheric voltage probe supplied by

Meteorologic Research of Pasadena, California—feeding into one of the amplifiers (checked by their own meter)—and a pair of monel metal rods, three feet apart on a north-south axis and leading into one of the amplifiers.

The output from all four amplifiers was fed into a four channel Leeds & Northrop recording meter. The latter prints a dot, indicating a voltage magnitude, at appropriate intervals, often enough to exhibit an almost continuous line. Needless to say, such an interrupted record is not adequate for true simultaneity of the four records, but for this study the rough approximation proved sufficient.

From the beginning an extraordinary correspondence in the four records appeared. The two trees, the air and the earth exhibited variations at approximately the same time. The magnitudes differed, but all four showed increases in the positivity of the 'hot' electrode at the same time.

The apparent simultaneity of two tree potentials, earth potentials and air potentials raises an interesting question. The short-time relationships between the onset of these changes in all four of these records could be exceedingly important. None of the equipment we had with us, however, made it possible for us to investigate this particular aspect of the problem.

Conceivably, the changes in the electrical environment might precede the changes in the electrical properties in the living systems. This would give added weight to the evidence that there is a significant relationship between endogenous electric characteristics of the two trees and the corresponding changes in the electrical aspect of the environment.

These short-time measurements were, of course, stimulating and interesting, but the really important question raised by this whole study is: What happens in time, preferably long periods of time?

A mathematical analysis of the diurnal rhythms made it clear that we were not dealing with random numbers but with real changes in the electric properties of a segment of the earth and of the two living systems. It seemed reasonably safe, therefore, to assume that both air and earth potentials were equally free from random measurements.

The fact that all four sets of measurements exhibited changes at the same time made it quite clear that a long-time study was justified. Since preliminary studies of this sort were begun in 1938, and reasonably continuous measurements made from 1943 on, quite a span of time was available for analysis. In the early days, mathematical theory was inadequate to study the changing relationships with time; and the modern mathematical analytical instruments were not available. The very considerable amount of data collected over the years represents a source of numbers which could be analysed very profitably.

5

Inspection of the potentials recorded on the long paper records made it clear that no one of these four sets of measurements was independent of the other three. A change in one was accompanied by a change in all the others.

This was an extraordinary finding. Every attempt was made to cover the possible artifacts which might have produced these results, but rigorous controls ruled out the possibility that the results were accidental. It must be admitted that it was exciting to see that the well-known diurnal rhythms of a biological system of two trees also were paralleled by diurnal rhythms in atmospheric potential and earth potential. To be sure, we do not know whether one or the other of these measurements precedes any of the others, but the fact that the changes occur in all of them is of prime importance.

Since Nature is the experimenter, changing the variables in both the living system and in its environment, long-term studies should help us to understand to what extent there is an interrelationship between the electrical properties in the environment and those of a living system. That they exist in day and night rhythms, is clear. But it is also equally clear that there is a repetitive cycle which has a period roughly approximating that of the lunar cycle.

This does not mean that the moon affects the living systems, as the old wives' tale held, but rather that both the moon and living systems respond to some more primary characteristics of the Cosmos. It is not surprising, therefore, that we detected in our records the same twenty-seven-day-cycle of earth and air, as well as trees.

Since these studies ran through many years, seasonal changes —which we know exist in trees, for example—were also to be seen in the winter and summer records of voltage gradients in earth and air. These seasonal changes were so obvious that the striking correlations between the living system and its environment gave credence to the notion that the living system is imbedded through its own electro-dynamic field in the field of its physical environment.

But since the field of the environment is involved in such things as lunar cycles, it is important to remember that the electrical properties of the ionosphere are changed by sun spot activity, as Stetson showed many years ago. The electrical characteristics of the ionosphere could, then, be correlated with lunar cycles and diurnal rhythms.

A preliminary analysis, therefore, was made of the changing potentials of the trees and sun spot activity as recorded in Zurich, Switzerland. *Here, again the correlation between the two sets of measurements was extraordinary.*

A great deal of further study will be required to determine whether or not the changing sun spot activity preceded the change in the electrical properties of trees. The graphs drawn from these available numbers show a rather extraordinary parallelism with the changing electric potentials of the tree.

By implication, this could indicate that not only a tree—a perfectly good living system—but in all probability all living systems, might show the same dependency since they all possess electro-dynamic fields.

There is a hint, furthermore—although this is by no means valid and final evidence—that the changing potentials of the tree follow, by a predictable amount of time, the changing relative sun spot numbers. As the sun spot numbers increase, voltage gradients in the trees increase. When the relative sun spot numbers decrease, there is a corresponding decrease in the voltage gradients in the trees.

Since the plots are derived from numbers scattered over an eleven-year cycle, and since there is good evidence to show that these electro-metric numbers in living systems are not random numbers but are valid evidences of changing electrical properties of a living system, it would seem possible to conclude with reasonable assurance that there is a close relationship between the electrical environment of the tree and the activities recorded electrically in the trees themselves. These changes could not possibly be the result of accidental correspondences. The numbers recorded are too great over too long a period of time to be chance observations.

It will be remembered that the primary assumption made at the outset of this study was that the electrical properties of a living system were evidence of an inherent electro-dynamic field. Since it is common knowledge that one field cannot exist within another field without an interaction between them, and the field properties of the ionosphere are modified by the bursts of sun spot activity, the effect on the electrical characteristics of the environment of the earth are really no more than might be expected.

It would seem reasonable to conclude, therefore, that a study of longer duration with more sources of information might make it abundantly clear that the field properties, not only of living systems but of the Universe, interact in characteristic fashions and produce results of great significance.

All this is of prime importance since we are now exploring space, which also must possess field properties. This badly-neglected aspect of environment study should be explored intensively. There is no reason why future plans to put recording instruments into space should not include adequate measures of field properties of the space through which the instruments pass. This, of course, would require highly-sophisticated instrumentation, very large sums of money and many studies.

But the evidence outlined above—while only a drop in the

bucket—nevertheless is highly exciting and interesting and gives us a clue to a hitherto-undreamed-of factor in the properties of the material Universe and of all living systems which exist within it. It may take many lifetimes, however, to come up with an answer which has genuine validity.

It can be argued that this is an extrapolation beyond the evidence. This is admitted. But these field properties are not mysterious phenomena; they are measurable characteristics not only of the Universe but of the immediate environment of the earth. Moreover, the evidence collected during the several decades of study indicates that the behaviour, in particular, of living systems is a consequence of the pattern of organization. And the arrangement of the charged particles in living systems is a consequence of the inherent electro-dynamic field.

These phenomena can be measured; and whether or not it is felt that the extrapolation suggested is beyond the evidence, there can be no question about the validity of the measurements. These have been checked over and over again, subjected to careful and critical mathematical analysis.* The present analysis would seem to suggest that we are dealing with valid, measurable interrelationships between the electrical properties of a living system, of all living systems, and the field of electrical environment in which they exist.

It has been the habit, in the past, to assume that a living system's behaviour is, in part, the consequence of chemical flux of the tissue of which living systems are made. However, the chemical flux is a widely and rapidly changing set of phenomena and yet throughout all these studies the constancy of the electrical phenomena is so great that they must be an evidence of some constancy in the growth and development of living systems. It is as though there were in every living system some guiding factor which not only makes the acorn grow into the oak tree but also induces a characteristic pattern of organization, of which

---

* Through the interest and diligence of Mr. Ralph Markson, a mathematical analysis of tree potentials was undertaken. With his consent, the results are printed in Part II starting on page 166. They add a very valuable and much needed mathematical validation of the important consequences of the Field Theory.

the physiological functional activities are known as behaviour.

To be sure the chemistry is of great importance, because this is the gasoline that makes the buggy go, but the chemistry of a living system does not determine the functional properties of a living system any more than changing the gas makes a Rolls-Royce out of a Ford. The chemistry provides the energy, but the electrical phenomena of the electro-dynamic field determine the direction in which energy flows within the living system. Therefore they are of prime importance in understanding the growth and development of all living things.

It must be remembered that this was an adventure into one of the frontiers of modern science. There have been, over the years, two major classical theories of modern science. One is best described as particle physics, where attention was paid to the unitary elements involved in any system under observation. The other can be subsumed under the general heading of field physics.

This was clearly enunciated many years ago by Clark Maxwell who, in his initial paper on electro-magnetic theory, noted that whereas particle physics was concerned with unitary elements or with what the Greeks called atoms, he called attention to the fact that the relationships of the entities were quite as important as the entities themselves.

As noted earlier, this was one of the reasons why we set out decades ago to see if by using methods of modern electrical measurement, we could examine these relationships as profitably as a study of the component parts themselves.

One of the key problems of modern science is that of organization or of that design of living systems which make it possible for us to define things in space and to describe the discernible patterns to be seen in the world around us. We are all familiar, of course, with the fact that descriptive science over the centuries has concerned itself primarily with little more than the straight description of the observable things on the face of the earth and, to some extent, in the heavens. Any description of these things in the world around us would not be possible if they were constantly changing their patterns.

Aristotle, moreover, called attention to the fact that an acorn always grew into an oak tree and not into a fig tree. This, of course, is the key biological problem. In other words, what is the nature of the forces which guide the growth and development of an acorn so that it ends up as a tree and not as a horse? These forces not only guide the growth of an acorn to an oak tree, but also determine the uniqueness of any particular oak tree.

Since this demands forces which operate in time and also show an astonishing constancy in spite of the chemical flux of metabolism, these must be studied from two points of view. One, of course, is to describe or define the chemical components of the biological system. Great strides have been made in the analysis of the chemistry of protoplasm and its constituent parts, but the rather extraordinary thing about it is that, fundamentally, there are only four chemical substances involved in protoplasm—carbon, oxygen, hydrogen and nitrogen. To be sure, there are additional trace elements in any chemical analysis of protoplasm, but the fact remains that these four relatively simple chemical substances can be arranged in incredibly complex sets of relationships.

Relationships must be the result of forces operating between the chemical constituents. These forces determine the position of these chemicals and their motion or movement in the process of growth and development. They eventually exhibit perhaps one of the most extraordinary aspects of this problem: they give some kind of *directive*.

They are not just haphazard interactions between the component entities but forces which apparently are involved in a directional control of growth and development. In other words, the forces have vector properties.

They not only control the interrelationships between the entities but they also control the direction in which the whole living system progresses. Among the aspects of nature capable of introducing direction are electrical properties—electro-magnetic, electro-dynamic, electro-static. With these, there is always

108

a direction in which the particles move. The motion is always between one pole and another of the environment.

This polar property and the control of the motion between the component parts can best be examined by electrical measurements. If, then, the observed electrical properties of protoplasm can give us a clue to the nature of the forces which impose organization on living systems—and, quite probably, on non-living systems—then a long-term study should offer at least some tentative conclusions regarding the interrelationships between the electrical properties of the living system, on the one hand, and of the environment, on the other.

*　　*　　*

That was the reasoning which originally prompted us to embark on continuous studies which occupied three decades. It is submitted that the exciting results obtained from our 'antennae to the Universe' fully justified not only the initial assumption but also this particular aspect of this adventure in science.

CHAPTER SEVEN

The Continuing Adventure

1

Though this adventure in science has occupied more than forty years, we have merely reached 'the end of the beginning', in Sir Winston Churchill's phrase. Each thing we have discovered in our long quest has shown us how much more remains to be discovered about the fields of life.

Nobody has recorded the feelings of the ancient Vikings when —after a long and arduous voyage—they came to the North American Continent. But, as they skirted a seemingly-endless coastline, it is safe to assume that their uppermost thought must have been that even greater adventures awaited those who one day would explore the vast territory they had found.

Similarly, the landfall we have made—for which we could only hope when first we set sail—gives promise of a vast area of virgin territory to be opened up by the scientists of the future. For if—as all the evidence has indicated—the fields of life are primary and control all living things we can set no limits to the scope they offer for further exploration.

As the scientists of the future acquire a more comprehensive knowledge of L-fields, they will gain a greater understanding not only of man's body, mind and behaviour and of the workings of all living things but also of the relationship between the fields of life and the greater fields and forces of the Universe. As astrophysicists learn more about the latter, biologists and doctors will be able to view the living things of this planet in a new and broader perspective.

In this, as in other branches of research, the scope for exploration seems as large as the Universe itself. This is not only because our knowledge of most things is deplorably incomplete but also because the organization of the Universe does not preclude change and development; on the contrary these seem to be inherent in it. The Universe is not static but almost inconceivably dynamic with everything in it—from galaxies to atoms—in a state of constant motion or change.

At the outset of this adventure we made the 'primitive assumption', based on all the evidence available, that we live in an ordered Universe. We assumed that order is imposed on the elementary components of Nature, whether particle or wave, by means of definite arrangements or patterns of organization which persist in time and which we can identify. We recognize these as permanent elements in the environment; we recognize trees and plants, birds and beasts, monkeys and man. If these patterns did not persist any description of the things we see would have no continuity.

On the other hand, we have only to look around to observe that no particular design, pattern or arrangement of parts ever appears at the outset full-blown or in its final form; there is always a developing process. The acorn grows and develops into an oak tree, never into a fig tree. It is obvious, therefore, that the laws of Nature do more than develop a pattern: they also determine the steps by which the pattern evolves, grows and develops. In other words, there is nothing fixed about the Universe; it is a growing active system.

It is a far cry from the most elementary living forms to the highly complex systems which have evolved from them. There is a great gap between the simple elements and the complicated, giant molecules which have been developed from them not only by Nature but also by man.

Man, in fact, imitates Nature in developing from the simple to the complex. For instance, he started by cooking and keeping himself warm with burning sticks; now he has the modern electrical kitchen and automatic heating systems. Simple screws and bolts, gears and wheels are organized into the marvellous tools and machines of today. And surely Henry Ford would be amazed at the modern automobile which developed from his Model T.

We cannot foresee the ultimate outcome either of Nature's developments or of man's. This makes the whole process of examining every aspect of the Universe an alive, exciting and adventurous exploration.

Yet, from time to time, some pundit will declare with solemn finality that there is nothing more to be discovered in his particular field of study. And almost invariably he will soon be made to look foolish by some new discovery or breakthrough which opens up new areas to explore. We can feel sorry for such self-satisfied people because these rash statements not only betray their lack of imagination but also show that they have missed one of the great adventures of life—examining a *developing* Universe.

We have no right to assume that the present state of the Universe is the final one, because all we know about it is that it has grown and developed over a vast span of time. And there is no reason to suppose that that development has come to an end with our present environment.

We cannot know the final end of growth and development, but at least we can be quite certain that it has an ultimate goal. It is doubtful, however, whether this ultimate goal is a fixed and final one; more likely, the goal itself develops with time. Perhaps the present is always moulding the future. For it is impossible to imagine that any of the material units of our environment are in final form, because everything we know is developing and growing towards a more perfect realization of the operation of the basic laws of the Universe. While we can make effective use of our growing knowledge of these laws, we have no way of predicting what the ultimate outcome will be.

2

In exploring a developing Universe, science's basic aim and problem is to determine the origin of its design. Science now knows a lot about the design itself but how it started is still shrouded in mystery. This central problem of science is of prime importance, not for mere academic reasons but because if we could know more about the origin of the Universe we might know more about how to conduct ourselves and our affairs.

At the present time, in the hope of solving that mystery, we are spending billions of dollars exploring space. The techniques which have made such explorations possible are almost beyond description. It is certainly a miraculous development, which may yield products of practical utility to mankind and which, for this reason, is quite possibly worth the money spent on it. But, so far, it has contributed little to man's understanding of the world in which he lives. And, as far as the basic problem of science is concerned, we are no wiser than we were before the Russians launched the first *sputnik* into space. The origin of the Universe still eludes us.

Perhaps it always will. In the meanwhile, however, we can learn more about something no less important—the forces which control *the unfolding of the design* of the Universe through growth and development. Of these, the fields of life are perhaps the most amenable to further study because—as has been shown in the preceding pages—they exist in all living forms so far examined and can be measured with great precision in controlled and repeatable experiments.

L-fields, therefore, offer us a new and scientific approach to some of the methods used by Nature to execute her designs. By studying these methods we can hope to learn more about the designs themselves, even if we remain unable to solve the great mystery of their origin. We can hope, too, to gain a greater understanding of how the designs fit in to the pattern of the larger designs of the Universe. For, as we noted in the first chapter, L-fields by their very nature must be influenced by the all-powerful fields of the Cosmos and must therefore be an integral part of its overall design.

Meanwhile, the fact that L-fields are a part of the Cosmic design is compelling evidence that we live in a Universe of law and order, because they *impose* design and organization on the constantly-changing material components of all living forms. They *compel* an acorn to grow into an oak tree—and only an oak tree; they *compel* a maize seed to grow into a corn-stalk and not a stalk of wheat or barley. Anything that *compels* growth and development in an organized way is irrefutable evidence of law and order.

But the L-fields of this planet are themselves influenced by the greater fields in which our world is enmeshed, as we found from the effects of sun-spot activity on the fields of trees. They are subject, then, to 'higher authority'—so to speak, which *compels* them to change in various ways. And, no doubt, the fields that surround this planet are themselves subject to the greater fields of space.

In other words, L-fields are links in a 'chain of authority'. This starts with the simplest living forms, runs upwards through all the life on this planet to the most complex form we know—man —and then extends outwards into space and upwards to an infinite, ultimate authority, about which we can only speculate.

This 'chain of authority', of course, does not apply only to the fields of life. It must also extend from the heart of the smallest atom to those gigantic forces which keep the planets in their orbits, which govern the stars in their courses and which regulate the feverish race of the most distant galaxies towards the outer reaches of space.

In building living forms, the fields of life override the normal laws of chemistry and physics. They compel atoms and molecules to assume—and to retain through constant changes of material —stable arrangements, which break down to simpler compounds after the death of the form. If it were not for this 'overriding authority' of the L-fields you and I could not exist in our present form because the complex molecules of which we are composed could not build themselves on their own—or by chance—and could not retain their composition.

You and I, then, are literally held together by definable laws, of which L-fields are a manifestation. Without these laws—or if the Universe were really chaos—we could not exist for a millisecond. Rigid, specific and exact forces control not only the construction and maintenance of our component parts but also their organization and interrelationship.

In short, we exist by virtue of inexorable laws in a highly-organized Universe of law and order.

3

All this will not appeal to those who prefer to believe that the Universe is chaos and man an accidental end-product of fortuitous chemistry. This view is enjoyed by those who like to imagine that man can do just what he pleases and that there are no laws to control his decisions to do this that or the other.

But, from the beginning of history, most of humanity has realized, however dimly, that there is some kind of law and authority in the Universe. This is shown by the fact that mankind—not knowing what that authority is—has postulated deities of many kinds and a Spiritual Universe in authority over the Material Universe.

The material and the spiritual, the body and the mind, the organism and the soul—these contrasting concepts represent a prevalent attitude of mankind towards the Universe in which he finds himself.

But is this attitude really justified? Is it merely the result of our lack of information about the true nature of things? If the Universe is one of law and order—as all the evidence indicates—is it not more likely that there is really a 'unified authority' rather than a 'divided rule' of the spiritual and material? Webster defines universe as: 'All created things viewed as constituting one system or whole; the creation, the cosmos.' The very word, then, implies unity, not the 'dual control' of two kinds of authority.

If, too, we accept that the Universe is one of law and order, are we justified in assuming that it includes some chaotic exceptions? Is it not more likely that such an assumption is merely a product of our ignorance?

The fields of life can offer us a new approach to these vital questions. But, before we discuss this, it is necessary to distinguish between the three kinds of laws that govern mankind:

First, there are Nature's laws, definable and reproducible, which, as far as we know, are valid right through the Universe. Though we can hope to learn more about them, it is certain that we can neither alter nor repeal them.

Second, there are man-made written laws which vary from country to country and from state to state. These—as we are painfully aware at the present time—are not always enforced or enforceable and can be argued, evaded or appealed *ad nauseam*. While Nature's laws are precise, inflexible and permanent, man-made laws are often fuzzy, pliable and variable. So much so, in fact, that it is hard for many who are only familiar with man-made laws to realize that there can be a superior kind.

Third, there are the so-called moral laws. These, again, are laws invented by the mind of man, nearly always with the hope that they will improve man's attitude towards other men. Most, if not all, of these laws are the product of the intuitive, creative capacity of the mind of man—expounded by the philosophers and prophets of past generations. They are valuable because, like the written law, they are primarily concerned with controlling behaviour and represent one creative activity of the mind of man. But they vary from country to country and bear little—if any— relationship to the laws of the Universe.

Moreover they have been imposed on mankind by tradition and by past intuitions; and it is hard to believe that the elder statesmen of two or three thousand years ago could present, through intuition—valuable as it may have been—the answers to *all* the questions which actually face the mind of man today.

Of the three kinds of laws, only those of Nature that we have discovered can give us a feeling of certainty. At the sub-atomic level, it is true, there is still some uncertainty. But once the sub-atomic entities are agglomerated into atoms or molecules we can recognize and validate primary laws and forces. We know, for example, that there is a law of gravity. We also know about electrical and magnetic forces, nuclear forces and contact forces. The laws underlying such phenomena, in fact, are so well known to scientists that they can be made to serve mankind. Our use of these natural laws in the present age is miraculous. As a result, we live in a much more comfortable world—at least in the Northern Hemisphere—than mankind has ever known.

Those parts of the world which we choose to call 'primitive' are so because their inhabitants have not yet learned enough about the laws and forces of Nature to use them to their full advantage. Through the extraordinary development of science, the Western world has put forces to work for its benefit in an exciting and unprecedented way. This would not have been possible if there were no natural laws and forces which the mind of man could discover and—more important—understand.

To the precise laws of Nature, man's written and moral laws offer a depressing contrast. The written law, formalized and expanded by lawyers, is not necessarily the law by which men live. The living law of human beings is mainly an unwritten law but it controls the major part of our activities. In many ways, most of us tend to ignore the written law and behave as we think commonsense, as it is called, dictates.

Moral law is even more flexible—as we see in the current era of 'permissiveness'. And it is always easier to tell the other man what he should do than it is to do those things ourselves. Man has an astonishing capacity to dodge the issues, to hide his real drive behind a plethora of words which, in many cases, serve as an excuse for what he thinks should be done or perhaps, more accurately, for what he wants to do.

It is an extraordinary fact that over the past few thousand years man has developed an astonishing capacity to use the laws of Nature for his benefit but, as far as one can see, he has not made a comparable advance by his use of the written or moral laws.

Most of man's troubles are spawned in the swamps of his own desires. And his written and moral laws have no relation to the laws of Nature. As a result, conflict, frustration and anxiety rule the minds of many, because they cannot reconcile their written and moral laws with the laws of Nature.

We will not be able to get rid of a great many of our troubles, therefore, until we attempt to relate the written and moral laws to the laws of the Universe. And if we spent the same amount of time and money on resolving the discrepancies between the man-made laws of the legalists and moralists and the laws of the Universe, there is no reason why our advances should not be as miraculous as those in our material environment. We need to devote the same kind of effort and thinking which is at present applied to space exploration to revise man-made laws and to harmonize them as far as we can with what we know about the laws of Nature.

4

No doubt it will take a very long time before we can make man-made laws more compatible with those of Nature. But it is important to make a start because the sooner we can do this, the sooner we can begin to resolve some of our problems and frustrations.

This task, of course, should be attacked from as many useful angles as we can think of. But in this book we can only consider the ways in which a further study of the fields of life can contribute to the greatest problem that faces mankind—human behaviour.

An immediate—and important—contribution which a knowledge of L-fields can make is the certainty that there *are* natural laws to which mankind is subject for us to discover and understand. We are not chasing a mere will-o'-the-wisp because we have found that the L-fields which control man are themselves subject to the greater fields of the Universe.

For us to get any real understanding of the nature of man and why he behaves as he does, it is necessary to find natural factors which, like the law of gravity, are valid everywhere and not only in the western, eastern or southern hemisphere. L-fields offer us a starting clue in this search because—as we have seen—the state of the human field reflects the state of the mind. As L-fields are subject to universal forces, operating everywhere, it seems reasonable to suppose that the latter have some planet-wide influence on the minds of men.

As extraterrestrial forces, such as solar flares and sun-spot activity, influence the L-fields of trees it seems most unlikely that human L-fields are unaffected by such forces. For instance, as this is written, we are approaching the peak of the current cycle of sun-spot activity. Is it coincidence that in the past few years there have been unusual world-wide unrest, riots and disturbances of various kinds? We do not know whether it is coincidence or not. But if we could establish by further experiment and analysis that mankind tends to be more excitable during increasing sun-spot activity, this knowledge, obviously, would be of the utmost value to world leaders.

No doubt other factors are involved in the present world-wide unrest but it would be helpful if we could recognize and isolate one of them.

The Foundation for the Study of Cycles, of Pittsburgh, Pennsylvania, has accumulated impressive statistical evidence that the affairs of man—from wars to hog-prices—seem to follow rhythmic cycles, though the Foundation has not yet discovered the cause.* Dr. Ravitz—as we noted in the first chapter—has found that the voltage gradients in the human L-field fluctuate in rhythmic cycles.

Are these phenomena in some way related to external forces influencing human behaviour through the L-field? Again we do not know but it would be useful to find out whether or not this is so. If it is—though we cannot control these external forces—it would be helpful to be able to predict periods when mankind is likely to be susceptible to wars or depressions.

Dr. Ravitz has shown that a study of voltage-rhythms in the L-field of the individual makes it possible to predict those times when his vitality and alertness are at a low point—times when he should avoid hazardous occupations as far as possible. Surely

---

*Since this was written, the Foundation for the Study of Cycles has republished (*Cycles*, January 1971) a paper, 'Physical Factors of the Historical Process' by Professor A. L. Tchijevsky, translated by Vladimir P. de Smitt. The paper was presented at the annual meeting of the American Meteorological Society in December 1926.

Professor Tchijevsky was Assistant, Astronomical Observatory; Collaborator, Institute of Biological Physics, and Fellow Archaeological Society, Moscow.

This scholarly paper deals with the influence of sun-spot activity upon human behaviour and the whole historical process; and gives some suggestive data and graphs. The Editor of *Cycles* describes it as a landmark in the literature. He comments that no conclusive case, pro or con, has been developed but that the task of establishing any relationship between sun-spots and human excitability is one of the more important unfinished projects of the Foundation.

it is not beyond the bounds of possibility that mankind—whatever the cause—is subject to *collective* 'lows' and 'highs'. If it could be determined that this is so, leaders would be able to know in advance those periods when they should exercise special caution, particularly in international relationships.

In these dangerous times, we cannot afford to overlook anything that might help to reduce risks. For this reason, a further study of these possibilities would seem to be justified. And with modern computers and techniques of statistical analysis such research should not be as expensive or difficult as further exploration of outer space and, quite possibly, might be of greater benefit to mankind.

5

Though it is important to learn more about the behaviour of mankind as a whole, it is no less important to study the human individual. For, however inconvenient it may be to theorists and bureaucrats, Nature has arranged that each of us is a unique individual. This cannot be too strongly emphasized in an age in which there is an increasing tendency to treat the essential individual as a mere statistic.

To anyone who has studied the human nervous system, however, it is clear that its nature is such that the incredibly-complex permutations and combinations of neurones result in many unique patterns of neural design. These neurones are located in particular parts of the nervous system and send branches to other parts of the nervous system.

Before the existence of L-fields was established it was hard to understand why a particular group of neurones should be lodged in the grey matter of the cortex and not in the spinal cord; and why the branches of the neurone—the dendrites and axones—apparently move to their ultimate destinations without mistake; normally, the neurone fibres which run to the ear never end in the little toe. The arrangements, therefore, of the neural parts is determined by forces which, we now know, are the electro-dynamic L-fields.

If this is accepted, the importance of field factors in the development and differentiation of the nervous system is evident. And it is no longer hard to understand how a neuroblast, developing and differentiating, should be located in a particular place in the primitive neural tube and why and how its branches should grow and be directed to an ultimate destination. It is not by accident, then, that the human nervous system, highly organized and very complex, should have such precision in its growth and development and such uniqueness as its final result.

All this is of great importance to students of human behaviour because it shows that it is not a consequence of local phenomena, nor the result of an endocrine or gastric function, nor of any other of the physiological properties of the living organism. Chemistry, whatever its origin, is a consequence—and not the cause—of behaviour.

To be sure, defects in behaviour can be recognized; this is well known. But chemistry can no more change an inferior nervous system into a better one than high-test gasoline can convert a Ford into a Rolls-Royce. Chemistry supplies the energy but it is the L-field which gives direction to the energy flow, the result of which is a pattern of organization.

Unfortunately, we know much too little about the consequences of the patterned neural mechanism in human beings. We know a little about the gross anatomy of the nervous system but we *know behaviour only through individual acts*. This leads to confusion in our understanding of the nervous system. We can only be certain that we are what we are not by accident but by a patterned organization or design, unique to each of us, which is regulated by a field.

It is true that there are certain patterns of behaviour and automatic responses common to all mankind, just as there are parts of the human nervous system to be found in other highly-organized nervous systems. Apart from these common factors, however, we are all different and behave differently.

Moreover, the mind of man has an unholy capacity to fool itself. We tend to see what we want to see, to hear what we want to hear. The raw data of sight, hearing, touch, taste, smell and so on reach the nervous system and become involved in the intricate organization of a linking and chaining together of nerve cells in the nervous system. These, as we know, number at least ten billion units and therefore provide an astronomical number of possible permutations and combinations.

These permutations, activated by stimuli from the outside world and also, unfortunately, from the inside world, determine in the last analysis what you and I do. This means, of course, that ideas are as powerful stimuli to the nervous system as the physical events in the immediate environment. These ideas have to be integrated with the raw data of sensation and also related to memory of past events before they result in overt activity.

Nearly everyone, when faced with the resulting problems wants someone to tell them the answers. This is not possible; no one else can tell you the answers which are right for you, though he may be able to help you, through ideas, to find the right answer for yourself. We should not and must not force our solutions on others, because each individual is different. We can only try, with suggestions, to help them to reach conclusions or solutions which are appropriate to their uniqueness.

Since we know no way to modify the field that determines the pattern of the human brain and the infinite permutations of neural response, there are definite limits to what we can hope to achieve in influencing human behaviour. Environment—a fashionable term at the present time—can undoubtedly be an extremely important factor. But it is clear that whatever we do to the human nervous system we cannot change its individual and inherent design determined by the field. Each individual is likely to react differently, even to the same environment.

Chemistry cannot help us. It is true that we can destroy—or produce a malfunction of—parts of the nervous system by means of drugs. They can often modify behaviour to some extent but this is only because they knock out one component so that another component can take over.

Similarly, certain operations on the brain can remove or short-circuit abnormal conditions and thus restrict undesirable behaviour. But they cannot alter the design. As a matter of fact, it is difficult for a brain surgeon to tell, merely by looking at the brain, what kind of person his patient is. There are some racial and age differences, to be sure, and brains vary in their size and weight. But no really significant differences have been found in the finer linking and chaining together of the neurones. This is not because they do not exist but because our present techniques are not adequate to unravel the complexities.

All this shows that—with our present knowledge at least—there are no instant cures for the defects of human behaviour. In other words we cannot hope to change human nature overnight, as wise men have always realized. Though this may seem to some a depressing conclusion it is better to realize our limitations than to entertain false hopes and to waste our energies in the wrong directions.

It is best, too, for educationists to realize that they cannot make a silk purse out of a sow's ear—that they cannot make a Beethoven or an Einstein out of a sow's-ear type of nervous system. The basic problem is to find out the capabilities of a particular nervous system and, by practice and experience, help it to develop into the most efficient apparatus possible for that particular and unique type.

6

All this is also relevant to the current demand—or hope—for a unified religion. Those who think this is possible are doomed to disappointment because we are all different and respond differently to the ideas which others suggest to us.

Religion can never be an organized set of regulations. It is a purely personal matter, depending on the human individual's reactions to his religious upbringing or teaching and to the ideas which may originate in his own mind about his relationship to what he believes to be the Designer, Organizer or Operator of the Universe.

It makes little difference what you call this qualitative attribute of the Universe—whether you call it God, or the Universal Mind or something else. The fact is that your relationship and mine with this thing outside ourselves—something which is greater than ourselves—is a purely personal matter between us and it, which cannot be organized or legislated by religious groups or in courts of law.

Since nobody knows the origin of the Universe, an infinite variety of opinions about its Originator is inevitable. Hence the enormous number of religious faiths and groups around the world, some of which appeal to vast numbers of individuals and some to a mere handful. It is often difficult to get general agreement on the interpretation of a set of facts. When there are no facts—in the accepted sense of the word—to interpret, it is obvious that general agreement among large numbers of different individuals is impossible.

Each individual, then, has to solve the problem of his relationship with the Originator for himself in order to reach a conclusion which is satisfying to him. There may be others who reach the same conclusions and also find them satisfying. But these should not be imposed on those who do not because, in the long run, each individual has to solve his own problems.

Nature revels in infinite variety. Far from trying to impose uniformity on mankind—or on anything else—she makes everything different. Our brains and bodies are all a little different from every other brain and body in the world. Even our fingerprints are different; among the many millions of fingerprints on file around the world, no two identical ones have ever been found—even among the many thousands of prints of 'identical' twins.*

L-fields are the tools which Nature uses to indulge her zest for variety; and we know no way to blunt them. In dealing with human nature, therefore, we should temper our idealism with realism and—like the wisest politicians—should confine ourselves to 'the art of the possible'.

In our modern civilization, of course, a certain amount of uniformity—in laws, regulations, procedures, printed forms and so on—is both necessary and unavoidable. But if we are to harmonize man-made laws with Nature's, we should neither seek—nor hope for—greater uniformity in regulating human conduct but should do our utmost to keep it to the minimum and, where possible, to reduce it.

It is the aim of some of the theorists and most of the dictators

---

* Confirmed by the F.B.I.

of this age to regulate the human race down to a dreary condition of mediocre uniformity. Perhaps, then, one of the most important things we can learn from the fields of life is that *in Nature precise organization and infinite variety can and do go together.*

We are likely to get further faster in the solution of our problems if we strive to imitate Nature, however difficult that may be.

7

Nobody knows what those early Vikings really expected to find when they set sail across the Atlantic. Perhaps they dreamed of fabulous and mysterious territory to conquer. But when they landed they found nothing too mysterious or unfamiliar—just a large and obvious continent to explore.

It has been much the same with our voyage of discovery. Whatever we expected to find out when we started, we have found nothing mysterious—nothing that need surprise us.

We knew before we started that, in the non-living world, fields and atoms are related attributes of matter and that neither can exist without the other. It was reasonable to suppose, then, that living systems—composed as they are of atoms and their fields—should contain electrical fields capable of determining the pattern of the structure and of maintaining it through constant changes of chemical flux.

This seemed the more likely because the electro-encephalograph and the electro-cardiograph had established the existence of electrical phenomena in living systems. And physicists know that wherever potential differences exist in conducting media currents flow and fields are the inevitable result.

The existence of L-fields, then, seemed as logical and probable as the existence of new lands across the ocean must have seemed to the Vikings. But, as with them, the problem was how to find the hoped-for goal. As with them, too, the goal was invisible. But here we had an advantage over the Vikings: we are accustomed in this age to dealing with the invisible.

We cannot see electro-magnetic fields but we not only know they exist but also put them to work for us in various ways. We have never seen electrons but we know how to use them. We know, too, that they are present in the nucleus of the atom; and it is perfectly clear that the properties of the atom are, in part interaction between the electrons and the whole atom and, in part, the contact which the atom has with other atoms. So, in contrast to the Vikings, we expected the result of our quest to be invisible.

Like them, however, we had to devise suitable equipment for our voyage of discovery. They had to build new ships to plough through stormy seas. We had to find new means to explore an ocean without causing any ripples on its surface—instruments which would draw no current from the organisms measured. As related earlier, this took three years; and it would be interesting to know if the Vikings were able to equip themselves more rapidly!

Though our goal seemed reasonable and attainable, it should be stressed that, when we started out *we had no certainty of reaching it*. However logical an hypothesis may seem, one can never be sure that it can be validated by experiment. The ships of scientific exploration can founder in the seas of experimental problems as easily as longboats can sink in the North Atlantic. But it is this element of uncertainty that gives zest to any voyage of discovery because, without it, there could be no hope of finding the unexpected.

Though, in any exploration, the unexpected is always welcome and exciting, the more clearly one can visualize in advance what one hopes to find, the easier it is to devise the right kind of experiment to validate the hypothesis. If one knows what one is looking for, too, there is less risk of wasting time down blind alleys.

We were fortunate, then, that our original hypothesis was sufficiently close to experimentally-demonstrable fact to save us from much wasted time and effort. We were lucky in the fact that science had reached a stage which justified the belief that electrical measurements of living forms could be made, that they would exhibit pattern and would serve as at least one measure of a controlling electrical field.

Over the years—as related in these pages—this belief has been justified by experiment. Wherever we made electrical measurements of living systems we found voltage gradients; and in all our experiments we found that the voltage gradients in living systems *without any exception* are organized in patterns. And the results of these many years of experimentation leave no reasonable doubt that *the field characteristic of a living system is a basic property of life.*

Moreover, since the field of a living system is an ordered pattern, it must be a part of the overall or general pattern which represents the Universe. It can be argued, therefore, that the Universe is an electrical field and that everything that exists in it is a subsidiary or component part of the total field.

This, of course, is not new. What is new is that it is now possible to make valid, repeatable measurements of the subsidiary fields which are associated with living forms. This shows that living systems are not some special creation—introduced into the Universe at some particular time or place—but are an integral part of the pattern—that is, of the law and order—of the Universe.

Someone once asked the question: 'What is this electricity which constitutes a field?'

A distinguished physicist gave the best answer that the author knows: 'Electricity is the way Nature behaves.'

This electricity, then, which can be measured and shown to have order and pattern, is not some strange and separate phenomenon but an essential characteristic of the Universe.

Numerous names have been given to these electrical fields. We refer to electro-magnetic fields, electro-static fields, and electro-dynamic fields and it used to be assumed that these are different and separate. This is not so. The various names derive from the instruments used to measure the fields. Thus, instruments which depend on magnetic forces would define the field as electro-magnetic, electro-static measuring instruments would define it as electro-static; those used in connection with the dynamic changes in living forms measure electro-dynamic fields.

The field, of course, is much more important than the instrument used to measure parts of it. It is a source of energy which can be visualized as controlling the organization of the Universe. Its electrical properties not only have magnitude but also directing qualities which determine the position of all the charges and give direction to the flow of energy.

8

When the ancient Greeks posed the question: 'Why is it that an acorn always grows into an oak tree and not into a fig tree?' they hit on the central problem of biology, which remained unsolved until modern instruments made it possible to measure the fields of life.

It had long been obvious to many biologists, of course, that evolution in general and particularly the evolution of the nervous system have had direction towards some ultimate end. One does not have to know very much about the human nervous system to realize that evolution has developed a responding system which is unique and which has the capacity for a high degree of discrimination.

If we consider the different levels of control of behaviour, it becomes clear that much of our behaviour is quite automatic, determined by the inherited pattern of the nervous system. This is true not only of neuromuscular mechanisms but also of those chemical activities of the body which are involved in the whole process of metabolism, both anabolism and catabolism.

On another level, there is the control of motor activity which can become automatic, as when we walk without thinking how we do it or use our arms and hands in various ways. Probably none of us really learned all that is involved in instructing our fingers to pick up a pencil and write a symbol on a piece of paper. In fact, if we stop to think about some action which has become automatic, such as tying a tie, we may bungle it. We acquire these skills by practice and experience and very soon they become automatic in the sense that they no longer require the conscious voluntary control of each muscle.

At the highest level there is a discriminative control—unique for each individual which, if he is reasonably 'normal', enables him to behave in what mankind chooses to call 'a rational way', and which is built almost entirely on discrimination of past and present experience. The human organism is unique on this planet because it possesses this highly-developed ability to discriminate.

It is impossible to imagine that the stage-by-stage development of the nervous system has happened by chance and without direction because *the ability to discriminate is the natural enemy of chance*. This highly-evolved ability, then, is further proof that you and I, as living organisms of the human type, are not what we are by accident.

If our nervous systems have not come into existence by accident, then they must have been developed by direction and organization. The experiments described in this book have demonstrated that field forces have the necessary qualifications for this task. We have seen, for instance, that they determine along which axis of the egg the frog's nervous system will grow and determine whether a seed will develop into a vigorous plant or otherwise. We have seen, too, that field-changes precede physical and mental conditions. All this is evidence of their organizing qualities, as there can be no organization without anticipation.

It is submitted, therefore, that we are fully justified in regarding the fields of life as the instruments of physical evolution, of which—on this planet at least—the human nervous system is the masterpiece. So, the more we study them, the more we can hope to learn about the nature of mankind.

9

You and I, then, are the products of a pattern of organization, or, to put it another way, the consequence of design. And it is very difficult to think of a piece of apparatus of any kind—whether it be an electric iron or an atom-smasher—that is not the product of the mind of a designer. Since, therefore, the Universe exhibits a design, it is not too much of a jump into outer space to assume that it is the product of a Designer.

As it is impossible to believe that the Universe has more than one Designer, the Universe is—as the word implies—a unit, set up and maintained by its electrical field. This all-embracing field is the creation and instrument of the Designer. You and I are part of that field and that design and not—as some like to suppose—accidental agglomerations of chaotic components.

With our limited knowledge of the field and our ignorance of its Designer it would be foolish to speculate about their nature. It is for each individual to reach a personal understanding of these things which satisfies his own unique requirements.

The primary value of the field concept is that it gives meaning for the Universe to you and me because design and organization imply not only direction but also purpose. This concept, too, offers a picture of the Universe which should be as acceptable as the law of gravity to many of different faiths, whether in the United States or Central Asia.

It in no way conflicts with any of those religions which teach that there is only one God. On the contrary, it reinforces their teaching by eliminating the need for two sets of laws in the Universe, material and spiritual. If we can accept that there is one Designer and one overall field, to which all humanity is subject, there is no longer any necessity to postulate one law for the material and another for the spiritual.

If the idea of two sets of laws could be eliminated, it should be easier for the human race to resolve some of its problems and disagreements. There is general agreement in all civilized countries about the law of gravity and other natural laws. But there are numerous—and sometimes violent—divergencies of opinion across the world about spiritual or moral laws; as this is written, for instance, there are religious riots in Northern Ireland. If it could be more widely accepted that the entire human race is subject to the same laws of the Universe and is a part of its purpose and destiny, it is at least possible that these disagreements would gradually diminish.

Even the laws devised by lawyers, which ostensibly reflect the 'conscience' of the community, may one day be brought into closer relation with the laws of Nature as that 'conscience' becomes less confused and variable.

This brings up the great problem of good and evil because lawyer-made laws are usually designed to maintain order and to control 'wrong-doing'. We know so little that we still have to think of good and evil as two opposite things; and we nearly always come a cropper when we try to define what is good and true and beautiful. Probably the only solid definition of what is 'good' is something that is valid or demonstrably true—something which is in harmony with known natural laws.

For instance, the law of gravity is demonstrably true and therefore legally and morally right. We accept that; and we do not regard it as 'evil' or to blame if a man defies it and falls off a cliff. Admittedly this is a first approximation to the problem. But it suggests the need to re-calibrate our concepts of 'good' and 'evil' by relating them to natural laws as far as we can.

Why is it that some of us do not conform to the environment in which we live and do things which are called bad or evil? We do not know the answer but, as we have seen, the design of the human nervous system permits incredibly-complex permutations and combinations, and it is activated by ideas, external and internal, which induce a great variety of responses.

Consider, for instance, the different neural responses to a beautiful piece of silver in a jeweller's window by two men, equally impoverished and in need of cash. One will wistfully admire its beauty and walk on; the other will smash the window, grab it and run to the nearest 'fence' to have it melted down. Their nervous systems have responded differently to the same stimulus.

Perhaps, as we learn more about the relationships between the L-field and the mind we may gain some insight into why people respond so differently to the same idea or impulse. Meanwhile, we can at least be certain that what we call 'good' and 'evil' are an inherent part of the design of the Universe—for what purpose we do not know—because there can be nothing outside that design.

Let us look over the log of our voyage of discovery and see what its results mean to you and to me:

Since you and I are components of the field of the Universe, we are all tied together in the same bundle of field properties. None of us can ever be independent of the universal field or of our own individual fields.

We are part of a designed whole which is not chaos but organized in law and order and which, over untold centuries, has slowly evolved the design and differentiation of the human nervous system. There is no reason to suppose that this is not also true of the Universe itself. It is extremely doubtful that it was created with one big bang and highly probable that it is still in the process of growth and development.

This is a slow process and we cannot hope to convert the Universe to our hopes or desires by tomorrow morning. We ourselves are the products of this slow process of growth and development and neither the great religious leaders, nor the great authors of pragmatic law nor any other factors that we know of can change or hasten it.

Though neither you nor I know the ultimate goal of the Universe in general or of man in particular, we can at least be certain that growth and differentiation are going on everywhere and all the time and that this process is not chaotic but has direction and an ultimate goal.

This gives meaning to our existence because we are a part of this process and because the process must have some purpose, even though we cannot discern what it is or see the end result.

Perhaps the purpose of the Designer is to observe, by experiment, the results of the reactions between field forces and material things, just as human organisms have to learn by experience and experiment. If this is so there is probably no such thing as an absolute set of values. The Universe is developing and so are we; and man's sense of values is likely to change as the Universe changes. What is true to the man of today will not necessarily be true to the man of tomorrow.

This seems the more likely when we remember that man's sense of values, of right and wrong, has always changed from generation to generation and from place to place.

It is exciting to reflect that life and the Universe are not static but active—evolving and searching for better ways to do things. And it is fortunate for mankind that there are no hard and fast answers to the problems of humanity. On the contrary, man has infinite scope to learn more about Nature's laws and to apply them to a better understanding of human behaviour.

*　　*　　*

The experimental findings recorded in these pages are the first stepping-stones on a long journey into the unknown— guide-posts for further adventures in science.

They indicate that the Universe is an ordered system, the human organism an ordered component. Law and order prevail from the biggest to the smallest; and to suggest that there is any chaos is merely to display our lack of information.

In short, the Universe has meaning and so have we. Though we do not understand it, the meaning is there. The continuing adventure of science and of ourselves is to seek, through the Field Concept, an ever-greater understanding of the changing, growing meaning of life.

PART II

Selected Papers

The author wishes to express his thanks to the authors listed above for their kind permission to publish their important papers in this book.

Appendix

Bibliography of H. S. Burr.

THE IMPLICATIONS OF THE ELECTRO-METRIC TEST IN CANCER OF THE FEMALE GENITAL TRACT*

Louis Langman, M.D., F.A.C.S.

(An investigation made in the Department of Obstetrics and Gynaecology, New York University, College of Medicine; Obstetrical and Gynaecological Service of the Third (N.Y.U.) Surgical Division, Bellevue Hospital)

In a former publication a technique (1) was described for measuring field forces in the intact human being. The hypothesis that cancer is fundamentally the result of an alteration of the organizational field forces in the living system was advanced. It was demonstrated that when measures of these field forces are properly made, obvious differences in the field properties of patients, with and without malignancy, can be determined. A polar reversal of the field forces between the cervix and the ventral abdominal wall was shown to exist in most patients with malignancy involving the female generative tract. Atypical growth in this system is accessible, it occurs all too frequently, and the diagnostic procedures while not perfect are reasonably adequate for recognition of cell morphology.

The technique as reported in an earlier paper made it possible to record the changes in voltage gradient which exists between the human cervix uteri and some indifferent point on the surface of the body, such as the skin of the lower abdomen. Thus, electrical changes in the intact organism with minimal disturbance in normal physiologic processes could be recorded.

* The gratitude of the author is hereby expressed to Professor Sebastian B. Littauer, Department of Industrial Engineering, Columbia University, New York, who was responsible for the statistical analysis of the findings presented in this paper.

The technique in brief consisted of a micro-voltmeter (a vacuum tube Wheatstone Bridge) connected through silver-silver chloride electrodes in physiological salt solution, on the one hand to the patient and on the other leading to a General Electric photoelectric recorder.* The reference or 'cold' electrode is held by a suitable bandage on the lower abdominal wall; the active or 'hot' electrode is introduced into the vagina until the tip comes to rest in the posterior fornix. The standing potential between these two leads appears on the recorder as a movement of the pen, either to the right or to the left of an arbitrary selected zero point. To the right indicates that the active electrode is positive to the reference electrode, movement to the left that it is negative to the reference electrode.

In a preliminary report (2) approximately half of the 30 cases reported were women with clinical evidence of malignancy, confirmed by pathological examination, and in whom a characteristic negativity of the cervix with respect to the lower abdominal wall was recorded. The remainder of the cases consisted of non-malignant conditions of the female generative tract including fibromyomata uteri, ovarian cysts, pelvic inflammatory disease, chronic cervicitis, and uterine bleeding due to a variety of causes. In contrast to the malignancies, all but three of this latter group showed a significant positivity of the cervix with respect to the lower abdominal wall.

In the more recent paper (1) the electro-metric observations in 428 women were reported. In 75 patients with known cancer of the female generative tract, 98.7% *showed the cervix to be consistently electro-negative to the ventral abdominal wall.* In 353 patients suffering from *non-malignant* conditions, 289 showed the cervix to be positive with respect to the abdomen (81.9%).

It was suggested that the electro-negativity of the cervix observed in the 64 patients with non-malignant conditions may represent an organizational weakness in the controls of growth

* Since this investigation was made more modern instruments have become available as described elsewhere in this book. These will make it easier to apply the electro-metric techniques described in this paper, as an aid in understanding cancer.

and differentiation in the organism in whom any one of a wide variety of stimuli may be sufficient to initiate atypical growth. The correlation of negativity with ovulation has been previously reported (3) so that if eight cases believed to be influenced by this process are excluded, this latter group can be reduced to 56.

SOURCE OF MATERIAL IN PRESENT STUDY:

The results of a continuation of this study extended to a larger group of women (860) have continued to show the same electro-metric difference between patients suffering from benign and malignant pelvic disease and suggests the possibility that this technique may be of value as a screening method in the detection of early malignancy in the pelvic organs of the female. A consideration of this possibility forms the basis of this communication.

The observations were made on women admitted to the Gynaecological Service in Bellevue Hospital and comprise successive admissions to the wards over a period of one and a half years. Some were admitted for diagnostic reasons, in others the diagnosis was clinically obvious. Nearly all had some gynaecological complaint. An attempt was made to study the electro-metric pattern in all women admitted with malignancy or suspected of having malignancy. Cases for study in the non-malignant group were selected at random. Normal women summarized in Table IV, represents a group of individuals comparable to those in a non-hospital population with no gynaecological abnormality. Medical technicians and a few of their friends comprise approximately 15% of this group.

Table I shows the observations on patients with pelvic malignancy according to age groups.

In all these cases the diagnosis of cancer was made after careful histological studies. During the period reported, electro-metric studies were made on nearly all patients admitted with a diagnosis of cancer or suspected of having cancer, regardless of the stage of the disease and in many instances, prior to the pathological diagnosis.

As is readily seen in Table I, a negative potential was recorded in all patients with malignancy except in five, for which no

TABLE I

ELECTRO-METRIC OBSERVATIONS IN PELVIC MALIGNANCY

DIAGNOSIS	AGE 21-30		AGE 31-40		AGE 41-50		AGE 51-60		AGE 61 and over		TOTALS
	POS	NEG	POS	NEG	POS	NEG	POS	NEG	POS	NEG	
Intra-epithelial*	0	2	0	2	0	1	0	1	0	1	7
Stage I	0	0	0	3	0	1	0	3	0	1	8
Stage II	1	0	1	2	0	3	1	5	0	6	19
Stage III	0	0	0	9	0	5	0	4	0	8	26
Stage IV	0	0	0	3	0	8	0	4	0	7	22
Adenocarcinoma	0	1	0	0	0	0	0	0	0	1	2
Carcinoma of Fundus	0	0	0	2	0	3	0	7	0	6	18
Carcinoma of Ovary	0	1	0	2	1	2	1	3	0	3	13
Carcinoma of Vagina	0	0	0	0	0	0	0	0	0	1	1
Carcinoma of Vulva	0	0	0	0	0	0	0	0	0	2	2
Sarcoma of Uterus	0	0	0	1	0	1	0	0	0	0	2
Metastatic Carcinoma	0	0	0	0	0	0	0	1	0	2	3

*Two additional cases of intra-epithelial carcinoma of the cervix have been studied electro-metrically subsequent to the cases recorded in this table. A positive potential was observed in one, and a negative potential in the other, so that in eight out of nine instances of intra-epithelial cancer a negative potential was recorded.

explanation is offered. Unusual malignant neoplasms are present in this group including one case of carcinoma of the bladder thought to be primary, one granulosa cell tumour of ovary, one dysgerminoma and a squamous cell carcinoma arising in a dermoid cyst, in all of whom a negative potential was observed. Of the five patients in whom a positive potential was observed, three were in women with epithelioma of the cervix, stage I and II, and two with ovarian carcinoma, one of which was recurrent, the other, involving both ovaries with marked ascites. The diagnosis of malignancy was clinically apparent in all five of these patients. *The fact that a negative potential was found in all of the cases diagnosed as intra-epithelial or preclinical cancer of the cervix except one, would seem to be of real significance.*

Disregarding the exceptions noted above, the results suggest that the technique may be of value as an aid in the early detection of malignancy in the cervix uteri, or in selecting those patients in whom further study to exclude the presence of malignancy seems indicated.

140

TABLE II
TABLE SHOWING ELECTRO-METRIC FINDINGS IN BENIGN CONDITIONS
WITH AGE DISTRIBUTION

DIAGNOSIS	AGE 10-20		AGE 21-30		AGE 31-40		AGE 41-50		AGE 51-60		AGE 61 and over	
	POS	NEG	POS	NEG	POS	NEG	POS	NEG	POS	NEG	POS	NEG
ibroids	0	0	17	3	59	6	35	6	2	4	1	2
id	17	1	58	2	28	3	2	3	0	0	0	0
Iogyn Pathology	5	0	43	0	14	0	7	1	3	2	2	1
regnancy	7	1	38	7	18	4	2	1	0	0	0	0
ervicitis	2	0	22	3	29	5	33	7	7	5	0	2
enign Ovarian Cysts	3	1	8	2	6	1	2	1	0	1	0	1
roliferative or Sec-etory Endometrium	2	1	20	1	22	2	17	1	1	2	0	0
Hyperplasia of Endometrium	2	0	4	1	3	0	7	2	3	1	0	0
Endometritis	0	1	8	0	5	0	0	0	0	1	0	0
Post Menopausal	0	0	0	0	0	0	0	0	10	10	0	1
ervical Polyps	0	0	2	2	1	0	3	0	0	1	0	3
ndometrial Polyps	2	0	3	0	4	2	2	1	2	2	0	0
vulation	0	0	0	3	0	5	0	1	0	0	0	0
ndometriosis	0	0	1	0	0	1	1	0	0	0	0	0
ranuloma of External enitalia	0	0	2	1	0	0	0	0	0	0	0	0
stulae	0	0	0	1	0	0	1	0	0	0	0	0
ranuloma of Cervix	0	1	0	1	0	1	0	0	0	0	0	0
trophic Vaginitis	0	0	0	0	0	0	0	0	0	0	0	2
ematrometria	0	0	0	0	1	0	0	0	0	0	0	0
eucoplakia	0	0	0	0	0	0	0	0	0	1	0	0

In considering the findings in patients with benign conditions, Table II, it should be understood that the diagnosis in all cases was based on histological examination of tissue. Attention has been called to the findings of negative potentials similar to the observations in cancer, which have been observed in women with post-menopausal bleeding in whom no morphological evidence of cancer was found. The next most frequent finding of negative potentials occurred in patients with chronic cervicitis where squamous metaplasia, marked in some, was reported. It is significant that in this group of patients, as in post-menopausal bleeding cases, the recording of negative potentials was more frequent in the older age groups where the incidence of cancer is greater.

Increasing knowledge of the behaviour of various types of tissue indicates that invasive cancer does not result from a sudden

TABLE III

ELECTRO-METRIC OBSERVATIONS AFTER OPERATION OR TREATMENT
PATIENTS WITH FOLLOW-UP

No.	ORIGINAL EMF FINDING	DIAGNOSIS	TREATMENT	EMF FOLLOW-UP
FW 41	1. 2/5/48 Neg.	Chr. cystic cerv. with squamous metap.	2/16/48 Vag. Hyster.	6/22/48 Pos.
ES 34	2. 7/23/47 Neg.	Chr. cerv, with squamous metap.	7/15/47 Total Hyster. Bilat. Salpingo-oophor.	12/16/47 Pos.
HH 36	3. 1/28/47 Pos.	Chr. endocerv, with squamous metap.	1/31/47 Total Hyster. Bilat. Salpingo-oophor.	12/11/47 Pos.
AH 48	4. 10/20/47 Neg.	Chr. endocerv.	10/22/47 D&C Removal of Stump	5/22/47 Neg.
BM 43	5. 10/16/47 Neg.	Carcinoma of Cervix	10/17/47 Radical Hyster. Bilat. Salpingo-oophor. Wertheim Radium 6720 hr.	6/23/47 Neg.
KC 46	6. 10/27/47 Neg.	Squamous cell carcinoma, Stage III	11/12/47 1800 Units 12/47 Radium 3360 mg. hr.	6/23/48 Neg.
MG 34	7. 3/4/47 Neg.	Carcinoma of cervix Stage II-III	Wertheim 5/26/47 X-ray 1800 Units. Radium colpostals and cork. 4320 ng. hr.	5/1/47 Neg. 7/7/47 Neg. 9/12/47 Neg. 2/26/48 Neg.
LJ 51	8. 11/19/47 Neg.	Squamous cell carcinoma, Stage II	Total Hyster. Post radiation. Atrophy of cervix. 1/22/47	2/4/47 Neg. (12 days after comp. hyster.)

MJ 9. 1/20/48 Neg. 50	CA of Fundus	Total Hyster. Bilat. Salpingo-oophor. 4/2/48	5/13/48 Neg.
BM 10. 10/8/48 Neg. 48	Sarcoma of Uterus	Supra-cerv. Hyster. Bilat. Salpingo-oophor 10/15/48	12/10/48
AJ 11. 8/21/48 Neg. 28	Intra-epithelial CA of Cerv. Stump following Supra-cerv. Hyst. Bilat. Salpingo-oophor 6/28/47	X-ray 8/18/47 6900 R. units. Radium 2760 mg.	9/29/47 Pos.
AS 12. 12/22/47 Pos. 33	Fibroids	Total Hyster. Left Salpingo-oophor. 5/12/48	5/18/47 Pos. 6/16/47 Pos.
RP 13. 5/6/48 **Neg.** 50	Intra-epithelial CA	Total Hyster. Bilat. Salpingo-oophor. 5/14/48	5/26/48 Pos.
MW 14. 4/19/47 Neg.	Intra-epithelial CA	Total Hyster. 4/25/47	10/28/48 Pos.
BL 15. 4/8/48 Neg.	Intra-epithelial CA	Total Hyster. Left Salpingo-oophor.	2/10/49 Pos.

metamorphosis, but is the result of a developmental process. The relationship squamous metaplasia has to carcinoma of the cervix uteri is currently controversial, so that the evaluation of the electro-metric findings with this condition cannot be definitive at the present time. Recent evidence (4, 5, 6, 7, 8, 9, 10, 11, 12, 13, and 14) indicates a localized phase of several years duration before cancer of the cervix becomes invasive. The observation of negative electro-metric findings in patients with squamous metaplasia of the cervix suggest the need for extended follow-up studies. Since the evidence suggests a significant correlation between negativity and malignancy, then all patients with negative polarity should be suspect and followed with great care.

For experimental purposes a correspondingly large group of cases with positive polarity should be observed over the same period in order to ascertain whether there is a significant difference between the two groups in the developmental rate of malignancy. Correlation of potential findings with morphological studies for a period of at least five years where no treatment has been instituted may determine the value of the electro-metric technique in anticipating those cases which will develop cancer.

The findings in patients who have had follow-up electro-metric studies (Table III) indicate that *a reversal in polarity from negative to positive occurs after total hysterectomy for intra-epithelial carcinoma of the cervix*. This reversal is not found in cases with more advanced stages of cervical carcinoma (Stages II and III), who have had either a radical operation or radium and X-ray therapy. Following a total hysterectomy, women in whom a diagnosis of squamous metaplasia of the cervix had been made pre-operatively, show a similar reversal in polarity.

These findings suggest that the electro-metric correlates result from causes inherent in the tissue involved and if the involved tissue can be removed in its entirety reversal in potential occurs. Conversely reversal does not occur when all the tissue involved is not removed by operation.

This finding may be of more than academic interest and may prove useful as one of the criteria for estimation of a cure. However, it is felt that sufficient follow-up studies have not been made both in number of cases followed and length of follow-up to

144

TABLE IV

SHOWING ELECTRO-METRIC FINDINGS IN WOMEN WITH NO GYNAE-
COLOGICAL CONDITION AND AGE DISTRIBUTION

AGE	POSITIVE	NEGATIVE	TOTAL
10-20	5	0	5
21-30	43	0	43
31-40	14	0	14
41-50	7	1	8
51-60	3	2	5
61 plus	2	1	3
Totals	74	4	78

TABLE V
MALIGNANT CONDITIONS
AGE DISTRIBUTION: ELECTRO-METRIC FINDINGS

AGE	POSITIVE	NEGATIVE	TOTAL
10-20	0	0	0
21-30	1	4	5
31-40	1	24	25
41-50	1	25	26
51-60	2	29	31
61 plus	0	36	36
Totals	5	118	123

TABLE VI
BENIGN CONDITIONS
AGE DISTRIBUTION: ELECTRO-METRIC FINDINGS

AGE	POSITIVE	NEGATIVE	TOTAL
10-20	40	6	46
21-30	229	27	256
31-40	194	29	223
41-50	116	24	140
51-60	29	29	58
61 plus	3	11	14
Totals	611	126	737

establish final conclusions. The problems inherent in follow-up
studies on patients cared for in Bellevue Hospital necessarily
limited the number that could be observed after discharge.

The significance of electro-metric recordings as a screening
method in large groups of normal women—better defined as

women presenting no gynaecological symptoms—becomes more apparent when we analyse the findings in women with no gynaecological condition, Table IV. In this group, 94·8% positive potentials were observed in striking contrast to women with malignancies in whom 95·9% negative potentials were recorded. (Table V.)

These observations indicate the necessity for further study with the identical technique for a large-scale type of experiment wherein electro-metric observations would be recorded on large groups of apparently healthy women—comparable to the women presenting themselves for examination in a cancer prevention clinic. The statistical analysis contained in this report substantiates the validity of such an experiment, in an attempt to establish the screening-value the technique may offer in women distributed in the general population.

While no definitive explanation for the findings presented in this paper can be offered at this time *the fact remains that electrical correlations in malignant and benign conditions have been discovered*. The application of this discovery as a screening technique in women with cancer of the generative tract is indicated from an analysis of the other observations made thus far.

The results of preliminary studies on cancer of the breast have shown similar electro-metric correlations and warrant further investigation. Similar studies in gastric malignancy (15), may prove of inestimable value in differentiating benign and malignant lesions in the stomach.

The technique should also be applied in an investigation of the prostate gland. Should such an investigation give 1 to 1 correlations in malignancy of the prostate similar to the findings in the female generative tract, a potentially valuable diagnostic aid in detecting early cancer of the prostate gland would be available. No other way of accomplishing this exists at the present time.

STATISTICAL DISCUSSION AND ANALYSIS OF FINDINGS :

An ideal medical test-procedure consists of a definitely specified sequence of acts such that the observations resulting can be unambiguously classified into a small number of distinct groups. A unique relationship between paired observations as exists, for

146

Table VII

COMPARING ELECTRO-METRIC FINDINGS WITH CYTOLOGICAL STUDIES
IN IDENTICAL PATIENTS WITH MALIGNANCY

PTS.	CELL STUDIES	ELECTRO-METRIC POTENTIAL	DIAGNOSIS
1. Y.A.	Normal cells	Negative	Carcinoma of Cervical stump, stage III
2. O.H.	Cancer cells	Positive	Carcinoma of Cervix, stage II
3. L.M.	Cancer cells	Negative	Intra-epithelial Carcinoma of Cervix
4. V.O.	Normal cells	Negative	Carcinoma of Cervix, treated, stage II
5. R.W.	Cancer cells	Negative	Carcinoma of Cervix, stage II
6. R.P.	Cancer cells	Negative	Intra-epithelial Carcinoma of Cervix
7. E.D.	Normal cells	Negative	Carcinoma of Cervix, stage IV
8. B.L.	Cancer cells	Negative	Carcinoma of Cervix, stage I
9. Q.G.	Cancer cells	Negative	Carcinoma of Cervix, stage I
10. F.W.	Cancer cells	Negative	Carcinoma of Cervix, stage III
11. P.S.	Cancer cells	Positive	Carcinoma of Cervix, stage II
12. M.E.	Normal cells	Negative	Carcinoma of Cervix, stage II
13. A.H.	Cancer cells	Negative	Carcinoma of Cervix, stage III
14. A.D.	Cancer cells	Negative	Intra-epithelial Cancer of Cervix
15. B.M.	Normal cells	Negative	Carcinoma of Cervix, treated
16. R.J.	Cancer cells	Positive	Carcinoma of Cervix, stage II
17. G.C.	Normal cells	Negative	Carcinoma of Cervix, treated
18. W.E.	Cancer cells	Negative	Carcinoma of Cervix, stage IV
19. A.F.	Normal cells	Negative	Carcinoma of Cervical Stump
20. A.F.	Cancer cells	Negative	Carcinoma of Cervix, stage IV
21. C.S.	Normal cells	Negative	Carcinoma of Cervix, stage II
22. E.M.	Normal cells	Negative	Carcinoma of Cervix, stage III
23. M.R.	Cancer cells	Negative	Carcinoma of Cervix, stage III
24. A.J.	Normal cells	Positive	Carcinoma of Ovary
25. L.V.	Cancer cells	Negative	Carcinoma of Ovary with extension to vagina
26. A.P.	Normal cells	Negative	Squamous cell carcinoma in dermoid cyst of Ovary
27. S.G.	Normal cells	Negative	Granulosa cell tumour of Ovary
28. Y.F.	Cancer cells	Negative	Adenocarcinoma of Corpus Uteri
29. M.D.	Cancer cells	Negative	Adenocarcinoma of Corpus Uteri
30. C.B.	Normal cells	Negative	Adenocarcinoma of Corpus Uteri
31. B.D.	Normal cells	Negative	Adenocarcinoma of Corpus Uteri
32. D.L.	Normal cells	Negative	Adenocarcinoma of Corpus Uteri
33. S.S.	Normal cells	Negative	Adenocarcinoma of Corpus Uteri
34. M.Mc.	Cancer cells	Negative	Carcinoma of Vagina
35. M.S.	Normal cells	Negative	Carcinoma of Bartholin's Gland
36. M.L.	Atypical	Negative	Endocervicitis
37 A.P.	Atypical	Negative	Chronic Cervicitis

example, in the presence of Koplick spots in the mucous membrane of the mouth prior to the skin eruption in measles is only too rare. Again the relationship from the Ascheim-Zondek test as an aid in the determination of pregnancy is so consistent (although not unique), that for all practical purposes, diagnosis can be made as though test results and the state of pregnancy were unique.

It is suggested that, similarly, a highly-consistent relationship exists between the state of tissue in the female generative tract, and the polarity revealed in the electro-metric test described above. The state of tissue as determined by morphological study of biopsy material is admittedly accurate. Were there a reasonable doubt in the interpretation of a sizeable percentage of such biopsies, then diagnosis could not be said to be reliable and the search for an adjuvant test would be meaningless. Hence inference about the reliability of the electro-metric test as an indicator of the presence of neoplastic tissue in the female generative tract is concerned only with the correlation between the polarity determined and the clinical and morphological diagnosis.

Electro-metric findings have been compared with cytology studies of smears from the cervix in the same patients, Table VII. This group is comprised of cases diagnosed morphologically as cancer, and consists of twenty-three cervical cancers; three of which were intra-epithelial or pre-invasive; four ovarian cancers, and six adenocarcinomas of the corpus uteri. Electro-metric observations and cell studies are consistent with the expected findings in malignancy in eleven cervical cancers, one ovarian carcinoma with extension to the vagina, two fundal carcinoma, and one primary cancer of the vagina. In three instances of cancer of the cervix a positive potential was recorded and cancer cells found on cytology study, while in nine cervical cancers a negative potential was observed and normal cells reported after cytology study. Negative potentials were recorded in four adenocarcinomas of the fundus in which normal cells were reported after cytology studies.

The evidence from this small group of cases indicates that electro-metric findings compare favourably with cytology studies as a means of detecting the presence of cancer in the cervix

148

uteri and may offer a more sensitive technique in uncovering cancer of the corpus uteri and ovaries.

Interpretation of the paired test results—clinical and electro-metric—is statistical. All measurements of human characteristics vary from person to person, although an examination of many observations shows that the 'thing' measured has a characteristic form, size, colour, or the like. That is, the 'thing' is identifiable, in spite of the fact that it varies from person to person.

Some human attributes are almost invariable, as for example the number of fingers on the hand, while yet the ratios of lengths of corresponding digits of the hand vary considerably. Height to weight ratios seems to show some consistency within a well established pattern of variation. Were, however, routine diagnosis decision-making are necessary if diagnosis is to be then a definite criterion statistically arrived at would be required. For it is obvious, indeed, that convincingly-verifiable criteria for diagnosis decision-making are necessary if diagnosis is to be made from the results of simple tests. It must be borne in mind also, that no matter how many people are subjected to a given test, they remain but a sample of the total population. Some assurance must be provided for the validity of the use of the test on the remainder of the population.

In order to infer a working principle from experimental evidence we require an accepted criterion of action. Suppose we state one of the results given above in the form of a working principle as follows:

Under conditions of the electro-metric test described above, negative potential is recorded in cases of malignancy involving the uterus or ovaries.

The statistical procedure followed in confirming such principles takes account of the sampling fluctuations of the observations. A provision is made for calculating the probability that, if the working principle be true, the observed results would be obtained, where the differences in the results are accounted for only by the random selection of persons to be tested.

For example, in the present case patients selected from a hospital population were chosen for electro-metric test. To be sure many of these patients possessed ailments of the generative tract,

149

Extended data (All these tables have 1 D.F. and Yates corr. was applied)

TABLE VIII
MALIGNANT-BENIGN AGAINST POLARITY FOR ALL AGE GROUPS

	MALIGNANT	BENIGN	TOTAL
Positive			
Observed	5 (a)	611 (b)	616 (a+b)
(Expected)	(88.1)	(527.9)	
Negative			
Observed	118 (c)	126 (d)	244 (c+d)
(Expected)	(34.9)	(209.1)	
TOTAL	123 (a+c)	737 (b+d)	860 (n)

Chi-Square: 318.5115

TABLE IX
MALIGNANT-BENIGN AGAINST POLARITY FOR AGE GROUPS 21-60

	MALIGNANT	BENIGN	TOTAL
Positive			
Observed	5	568	573
Expected	65.25	507.25	
Negative			
Observed	82	109	191
Expected	21.75	169.25	
TOTAL	87	677	764

Chi-Square: 171.2262

TABLE X
MALIGNANT-BENIGN AGAINST POLARITY FOR AGE GROUPS 21-40

	MALIGNANT	BENIGN	TOTAL
Positive			
Observed	2	423	425
Expected	25	400	
Negative			
Observed	28	56	84
Expected	5	79	
TOTAL	30	479	509

Chi-Square: 131.1986

TABLE XI

MALIGNANT-BENIGN AGAINST POLARITY FOR AGE GROUPS 41-60

	MALIGNANT	BENIGN	TOTAL
Positive			
Observed	3	145	148
Expected	33	115	
Negative			
Observed	54	53	207
Expected	24	83	
TOTAL	57	198	255

Chi-Square: 80.6839

but there was no way of knowing in advance what the recorded potential might be. Furthermore, the clinical examination and findings were made by physicians unaware of the results of the test so that no unconscious biasing of results was possible. What the statistical criterion does is to rule on whether the correlation between malignancy and negative potential is real and not the result of chance variations in the sign of the potential recorded.

The analysis of the results in Tables V and VI is made as follows: first they are transferred to Table VIII. In this table which contains the results of 860 tests on patients in all age groups, comparison is made of the distribution of polarity between malignant and benign groups and that in the total group. That is, the total group of 860 patients consists of 123 cases diagnosed as malignant and 737 found to be benign. We can also look upon this group of data as consisting of 616 positive potential recordings and 244 negative recordings.

The question to be answered is, 'is the potential recorded related to the condition of the patient, or is it distributed by chance?'

If the potential recorded from electro-metric test had nothing to do with malignancy of the fundus, cervix, or ovaries, then the expected number of negatives observed in the total group would depend upon the ratio of the number of negatives observed in the total group of 860 patients. According to Table VIII the expected values of malignancy showing positive should be 88·1 while those showing negative should be 34·9. On the other hand

151

the observed results show that 118 of the malignancies recorded negative potentials. Similar observations can be made on the benign cases.

We can look upon these results another way: The population of 860 cases can be grouped in two ways: according to the existence of malignancy or not and according to the polarity recorded from the electro-metric test. Then the question is raised, are the two groupings independent of one another? If the assertion that the two groupings are independent is shown to be highly improbable, the conclusion can be safely reached that there is a significant correlation between negativity and malignancy.

The criterion for this is the chi-square statistic calculated from Table VIII as follows:

$$\text{chi-square} = \frac{(\,|\,ad-bc\,|\,-n/2)^2 n}{(a+b)(c+d)(a+c)(b+d)} = 318.5$$

If the two groupings were independent then the ratio $a:c=b:d$ and $ad-bc=0$, and under these circumstances chi-square for a given set of observations could take on different positive values as the result of chance. The value 318.5, however, could occur by chance less than once in a million trials, whence it is argued that potential polarity and morphology of tissues are correlated.

The importance of these results lies in their use as a screening test. It is admittedly a time consuming and expensive task to make clinical examinations which include microscopic examination of biopsy material. *The electro-metric test can be recorded routinely by qualified technicians, at the rate of five per hour per instrument. Large scale testing can be planned at a low unit cost.*

The present results strongly indicate that the presence of neoplastic tissue can be discovered in a large proportion of patients. Many of the negative potentials recorded will not mean malignancy, but 95% of the malignancies should be uncovered as the result of finding negative potentials.

Hence we have this situation, which we can conclude from the results: in testing the general female population, most cases of malignancy of the generative tract will be discovered, while a large fraction of the cases recording negative potential will be benign.

If the coverage of the general population is the ideal desired the present test promises to reduce the requirement of highly specialized examinations to a small fraction of the total population.

Let us now consider the strength of the correlations. This question is not answered in a definitive way in current statistical methodology but in the present case the correlation is so marked that simple statistical tests can be applied to indicate the degree of correlation quite accurately.

In the present study,* unless we are the victims of a rare event, *in nine out of ten cases of malignancy, negative potential has been recorded.*

This is not the place to go deeply into the consideration of statistical tests. We do, however, offer Tables IX, X, XI and the chi-square values calculated therefrom which show conclusively that whatever age groups we chose, the correlation is definitely significant.

Use of the electro-metric test on a large scale should be made only after a careful statistical design. It is necessary that such an investigation permit quantitative evaluation of the results. Such a statistical design is currently being planned.

REFERENCES

1. Langman, Louis, and Burr, H. S. *Amer. J. Obst. and Gyn.*, 1949, 57: 274.
2. Langman, Louis, and Burr, H. S. *Science*, 1947, 105: 209.
3. Langman, Louis, and Burr, H. S. *Amer. J. Obst. and Gyn.*, 1942, 44: 23.
4. Graves, Wm. *Surg., Gyn. and Obst.*, 1933, 56: 317.
5. Pund, E. R., and Auerbach, S. H. *J. A. M. A.*, 1946, 131: 960.
6. Studdiford, Wm. E. Personal Communication.
7. Taylor, H. C., Jr., and Guyer, H. B. *Amer. J. Obst. and Gyn.*, 1946, 52: 451.

* The assistance of Miss Hannah Oren and Dr. Leon N. Greene is acknowledged with thanks.

8. Goldberger, M. A., and Mintz, N. J. *Mt. Sinai Hosp.*, 1947, 14: 784.
9. Te Linde, R. W., and Galvin, G. *Amer. J. Obst. and Gyn.*, 1947, 48: 784.
10. Knight, R. van Dyck. *Amer. J. Obst. and Gyn.*, 1943, 46: 333.
11. Rubin, I. C. J. *Mt. Sinai Hosp.*, 1945, 12: 607.
12. Smith, G. van S., and Pemberton, F A. *Surg., Gyn. and Obst.* 1934, 59: 1.
13. Stevenson, C. S., and Scipiades, E., Jr. *Surg., Gyn. and Obst.*, 1938, 66: 822.
14. Younge, P. A. *Arch. Path.*, 1939, 27: 804.
15. Goodman, E. N. Personal Communication.

ELECTRO-MAGNETIC FIELD MONITORING OF CHANGING STATE-FUNCTION, INCLUDING HYPNOTIC STATES*

Leonard J. Ravitz, M.S., M.D., F.R.S.H.†

1

The abysmal lack of growth, particularly in the United States, of true scientific breakthroughs in the social sciences may perhaps be related to a neglected historic fact: no basic scientific advances have stemmed from any pragmatic emphasis either on directly sensed natural history data or on directly sensed operational procedures. Yet if one is to gain any glimmer of understanding of man, it would seem proper first to ask fundamental questions of Old Mother Nature. Contrary to basic assumptions implicit in most of the currently fashionable approaches, man is part and parcel of nature, a meticulously designed product exhibiting the same inorganic constituents found in nature. The glob of protoplasm that develops into the optic nerve, for instance, seldom loses its way to end up at the big toe. To

* Condensed from a paper presented at Vth International Congress for Hypnosis and Psychosomatic Medicine, Johannes Gutenberg University, D6500 Mainz/Germany, May 22, 1970. Published in *Journal of American Society of Psychosomatic Dentistry and Medicine*, Vol. 17, No. 4, 1970.

† Diplomate, American Board of Psychiatry and Neurology; Special Medical Consultant, Frederick Military Academy; Consultant, Virginia Department of Health; Fellow, New York Academy of Sciences; Fellow, American Psychiatric Association; Charter Fellow, American Society of Clinical Hypnosis, President, Virginia Section; Fellow, American Association for the Advancement of Science. Fellow, Royal Society of Health. Graduate of Western Reserve, Wayne, and Yale Universities; formerly on faculties of Yale, Duke, and University of Pennsylvania Schools of Medicine. Member, Sigma Xi; President's Committee for Handicapped.

be sure we have facile explanations in terms of conventional mechanical and chemical tropisms. And did not Bergson and Driesch coin *élans vitals* and entelechies—supernatural agents defying scientific analyses which could sit on top of cells and tell them what to do? Cells belonging to special creations, *in* this universe but not *of* it, obeying their own special man-made laws, expanded by Freud into complex pluralistic interactions of mystical mental parts and mental forces.

Yet true knowledge of any subject matter cannot progress either by shifting terminology or creating supernatural factors whose very existence is guaranteed only by sheer acts of faith.

As Dr. Burr has described in the preceding pages, instruments have found what he and Dr. Northrop postulated over thirty years ago. Countless experiments have demonstrated that the electric fields they discovered serve basic functions, controlling growth and morphogenesis, maintenance and repair of living things. Naturally, these differ from the alternating-current electric output of the brain and heart, as well as from the epiphenomenal skin-resistance, serving rather as an electronic matrix to keep the corporal form in shape.

Obviously such studies throw a wet blanket on scientific dogma currently in vogue, which still asserts that the special human body is principally a chemical product deriving from mystical activities of the DNA molecule. However disquieting, chemistry represents a scalar property—the downhill flow of energy—requiring some vector force to give it direction. According to Dr. Henry Margenau, Eugene Higgins Professor of Physics and Natural Philosophy at Yale University, of all the known forces it is only electro-magnetic, or electro-dynamic, fields which can act as signposts to direct such continuous chemical, metabolic, or molecular transformations in the system—fields which, in fact, appear to underwrite the development of structure even prior to any known chemical reactions. That such field measurements can be related to energy seems obvious, natural energy which directs and/or misdirects the behaviour of living systems in a continuous stream of flux and reflux.

*　　*　　*

As an objective, reproducible, quantifiable, measurable clue to basic biologic processes seemed to be at hand, operating independently of current flow or resistance changes, it was logical to extend such experiments to longitudinal studies of human subjects in health and disease, experiments which through use of this new amplifier could also possibly shed light on the heretofore inexplicable phenomena of 'hypnosis'. Despite the profound physiologic changes in the system that can obtain from hypnotic states, hypnosis had continued to elude any objective, quantifiable, reproducible measure, even with the EEG and with secondary skin-resistance changes, notorious for their general irreproducibility and unreliability.

2

On April 24, 1948, at Yale University School of Medicine, *hypnosis was electro-metrically recorded for the first time and compared with field shifts during other state changes.* As hypnotic states themselves involve electro-magnetic flux and reflux, Maxwell's equations can be blamed for inadvertently resurrecting that much maligned ghost, Mesmer's 'animal magnetism', now more suitably based on the laws of modern field physics.

Soon afterwards another noteworthy discovery was made. Despite the numerous variables indigenous to living things in general and human beings in particular, *long-range studies on human subjects showed electro-cyclic phenomena identical to those of trees and other forms of life, but introducing a fortnightly rhythm.*

From over 50,000 field determinations on some 500 human subjects at several locations, including Yale, Duke, and the University of Pennsylvania schools of medicine, it has been evident since 1948 that such periodic movements provide objective profiles of variations in feeling and behaviour states which often transcend observable criteria. Despite the naïveté of applying linear-dimensional statistical analyses to non-linear organisms operating on multidimensional continua of uniquely determinable, continuously unfolding states, the highest known correlates

157

have been obtained between any physiologic measuring technique and estimates of symptoms. Ranging from states of excitation to states of exhaustion, electro-cyclic phenomena also open the door to both long- and short-range predictions.

With regard to human experimental studies in which subjects serve as their own controls, one of the initial approaches compared shifts in individual states before and after hypnosis along with effects of hypnosis as recorded and studied. Hypnotic and posthypnotic changes were then compared with corresponding field alterations. Disquietudes of all sorts induced in so doing have been studied electro-metrically and compared with those arising spontaneously both in waking and in hypnotic states. Further, changes have been measured before, during, and after various drugs and placebos, and proper dosages to achieve effects correlated with field intensities and polarities at given times. Similar experiments have likewise been conducted on effects of subjecting controls and patients to several therapeutic procedures.

In brief, subjects in trance states, induced or spontaneous, show a smoothing of the field recording and usually a slow decrease, although sometimes an increase, in intensity. At trance termination dramatic voltage shifts occur, the time before the record returns to that of the waking state depending on the rapidity with which the subject returns to the waking state. Subjects who have been aroused from trance states, but who actually are only partially aroused or return to the trance state though superficially appearing 'awake', show field correlates with such state changes, either by using pen-writing photo-electric recorders or cathode-ray oscillographs attached to the millivolt-meters, now commercially manufactured. (This was first publicly demonstrated at the Second Annual Scientific Assembly of the American Society of Clinical Hypnosis in 1959.) Waking states show almost continuous, slow variations, usually at higher intensities than during hypnosis.

It follows that hypnotic depth can now be defined electro-metrically, the 'depth', however, having nothing whatever to do with abilities to develop various complex hypnotic phenomena.

158

3

It is important to note carefully the neuromuscular and other changes in subjects characteristic of trance states, which Dr. Milton Erickson has emphasized and to which few have paid any attention. Ocular fixation, pupillary changes, sclerae alterations, altered eye-blink reflexes, muscular rigidity, including set facial expressions, have been noted to occur spontaneously in numerous individuals at certain times, persons who disclaimed ever having been 'hypnotized'.

The measurement of such persons after such physiologic alterations have been noted has without fail produced field records indistinguishable from trance states induced by a so-called 'hypnotist'. Almost invariably such individuals, when questioned, indicated that they were thinking about something at the time. This suggests, at the very least, that individuals go into trance states spontaneously and automatically during certain stages of intense concentration without necessarily recognizing them as such. Also, as Erickson long has claimed, carrying out post-hypnotic suggestions re-establishes the trance state as electro-metrically measured.

Such findings are of crucial importance in experimental work claiming to study ostensibly erudite groupings of 'scientifically observed' subjects supposedly hypnotized *versus* those who, because they have not been subjected to some ritualistic induction procedure, are thought to be in waking states. The spuriousness of such 'scientific' experiments is further evidenced when the experimenters are not really conversant with all the observable nuances of trance states, including the previously noted neuromuscular changes. Recognition of such state changes is especially important to those interested in obtaining waking-state field records, as the voltage changes accompanying hypnosis may be most profound.

This suggests a need to revise empiric definitions of hypnosis to include state changes that are not necessarily dependent on any 'hypnotist'—a fact with intriguing legal implications.

When they decrease in voltage, field records during sleep are indistinguishable from those during hypnosis. However, EEG changes are notorious for their absence during hypnosis, a predictable fact if one considers that higher discriminatory functioning can occur during hypnosis, whereas EEG alterations occur during sleep.

In 1958 the field basis of hypnosis was proposed by this writer, a derivative construct based on knowledge of various states which do and do not produce field variations, with or without concomitant EEG changes. This knowledge suggests that hypnosis represents a natural change in state function involving shifts in the balance of the phylogenetically ancient basal ganglia with respect to the phylogenetically recent cortex, in which field properties of the entire body participate.

Electro-magnetic field correlates of somatic and emotional disturbances in both waking and trance states are identical. What happens is in part a function of the state of the subject at any given time. If the initial energy or voltage level is low, changes may not be sufficient to be reflected to any great degree on the body surface. Yet field correlates of difficulties in producing hetero- or autohypnotic states at those periods when the variable baseline states are at high intensities suggest why acutely disturbed persons in relative states of excitation are difficult to hypnotize.

4

To summarize some of the other findings:

1. Barbiturate narcosis evokes minimal field changes and maximal EEG alterations, as do certain stimulants and depressants, e.g., caffeine, alcohol, etc.

2. Somatic symptoms show correlates especially with the polarity quantity, the 'high-minus' field configurations notable also in preadolescent and ageing adult groups. Certain periodic clinical conditions, e.g., peptic ulcer and allergies, show 1 : 1 correlations with the seasonal electro-cyclic shifts.

3. In clinically diagnosed schizophrenic patients voltage patterns range from the highest to the lowest intensities found. The

greatest field strengths, *states of excitation*, occur, regardless of apparent duration of malfunctioning, until about middle age in the forties. Improvement is preceded by, or correlated with, sustained voltage drops of greater stability, and polarity may also be reversed. The lowest field strengths, *states of exhaustion*, are usually observed in chronic inert patients. The most dramatic voltage rises have preceded those rare occasions when torpid schizophrenic behaviour shifts into animated, spontaneous functioning. Since exaggerated or inhibited behaviour is found with high field intensifications and as exhausted behaviour may *resemble* inhibited behaviour, the field profile is necessary to indicate objectively what is going on.

In 1956, at the Annual Meeting of the American Psychiatric Association, the phylogenetic basis of behaviour disorders was presented, a construct deriving from considerations of basic behaviour changes paralleling the evolution of the nervous system. Space will not permit even a statement of this theory here. Suffice it to say, all behaviour disorders not perverted by culturally false notions of 'normal' reflect, by this construct, an imbalance in the harmonious integration of the old and new parts of the brain.

4. Adult human subjects, as well as other forms of life, run downhill electrically with age, undergoing polar reversals into minus polarity, depending on the electrode placement, an entirely relative matter. Field profiles of infants and preadolescent children likewise have shown predominantly minus polarity. Typical Caucasian men during adolescence and early adulthood tend to show moderately high intensities of almost uniformly plus polarity. Caucasian women, on the other hand, dip minus much earlier than men. Pilot studies suggest that, aside from the unique design of each individual, inherent racial differences may be of prime significance in determining intensity, variability, and polarity at various ages. Orientals showing more minus readings than Caucasians of the same age, Negroes exhibiting far greater field intensification of plus polarity.

5

In summary, electro-dynamic field constructs add fuel to the assumption *unifying living matter harmoniously with the operations of nature*, postulating that each biologic thing is organized by a total dynamic pattern, the expression of an electro-magnetic field no less than non-living systems; and that as points on spectrums, these two entities may at last take their positions in the organization of the universe in a way both explicable and rational. Light has been shed on several heretofore elusive facts in many realms of knowledge. A tenable theory has been provided for emergence of the nervous system, developing not from functional demands, but instead deriving as a result of dynamic forces imposed on cell groups by the total field pattern.

Living matter now has a definition of state based on relativity field physics, through which it has been possible to detect a measurable property of total state function. Since 1948 this for the first time has included an objective, reproducible, quantitative measure of hypnotic states which can and do arise spontaneously, the depth of which can be objectively measured.

This has nothing to do with conventional depth scales. Hypnosis emerges as a natural field phenomenon which can be independent of any 'hypnotist', occurring when anyone is concentrating, thus discarding many experiments on hypnotized versus non-hypnotized subjects that do not first ascertain whether non-hypnotized subjects were in spontaneous hypnotic states.

Irreducible factors in the causation of behaviour and somatic disorders have been discovered, the behaviour perturbations favouring the intensity factor, the somatic disorders emphasizing the polarity vector. Hypnosis as well as health and disease and ageing have thus been measured in terms of changing intensities and directions of natural energy, an approach fusing the time-factor, or electro-cyclic phenomena, to the assessment of all living things pervading the entire phylogenetic tree.

Thus, a significant wedge has been driven into the problem of known periodicities in certain clinical conditions, as well as the obvious energy of youth, the profound and protracted disorders frequently arising in older-age groups, and the natural essence of 'hypnosis' itself.

During longitudinal studies of patients and controls several infectious diseases have been monitored inadvertently, reinforcing the importance of the field quantity as a unique property for each individual at any given time, continuously changing in accord with specific electro-cyclic periods. It appears, therefore, as though an objective measure of those properties of protoplasmic organization which establish the essential attributes of feeling, behaviour, and thinking has emerged. based on non-mechanistic causality principles.

As F. L. Kunz, Editor of *Main Currents in Modern Thought,* pointed out in his preface to a commemorative issue on the Electro-dynamic Theory of Life in 1962:

> The moment is propitious: we may be close upon the kind of breakthrough in biologic science which has brought the physical sciences to their present degree of control and refinement. If so, the implications for education, and indeed for all socio-cultural aspects of human life, are without precedent.

BIBLIOGRAPHY

1. A complete bibliography of the papers of H. S. Burr will be found in the Appendix.
2. Erickson, M. H. *Advanced techniques of hypnosis and therapy*: selected papers of, J. Haley, Ed. New York and London: Grune & Stratton, 1967.
3. King, C. D. Electro-metric studies of sleep. *J. Gen. Psychol.*, 1946, 25: 131-159.
4. Lund, E. J. *Bioelectric fields and growth* (with a bibliography of continuous bioelectric currents and bioelectric fields in animals and plants by H. F. Rosene). Austin, Texas: University of Texas Press, 1947.
5. *Main currents in modern thought.* Vol 19. No. I Sept.-Oct. 1962. Special commemorative issue on certain works of H. S. Burr, F. S. C. Northrop, and L. J. Ravitz. *The reality of the non-material cosmos and its relation to the sensed world of ordinary experience.*
6. Margenau, H. Particle and field concepts in biology. *Sc. Monthly*, 1947, 64: 225-231.
7. Margenau, H. Causality; 19·9, causation in biology, 415-418. In *The nature of physical reality*. New York: McGraw Hill, 1950.
8. Nelson, O. E., Jr., and Burr, H. S. Growth correlates of electro-motive forces in maize seeds. *Proc. Natl. Acad. Sc.*, U.S., 1946, 32: 73-84.
9. Northrop, F. S. C. The living organism. In *Science and first principles*, ch. 4. New York: Macmillan, 1931.
10. Northrop, F. S. C. The method and theories of physical science in their bearing upon biological organization. In *The logic of the sciences and the humanities*, 133-168. New York: Macmillan, 1947.
11. Ravitz, L. J. Electro-metric correlates of the hypnotic state. *Science*, 1950, 112: 341-342.
12. Ravitz, L. J. Standing potential correlates of hypnosis and narcosis. A.M.A. *Arch. Neurol. Psychiat.*, 1951, 65: 413-436.

13. Ravitz, L. J. Daily variations of standing potential differences in human subjects: preliminary report. *Yale J. Biol. Med.,* 1951, 24: 22-25.

14. Ravitz, L. J. Fenomenos electrociclicos y estados emocionales. *Arch. Med. Intern. Antibiot. Quimiot.,* 1952, 2: 217-253.

15. Ravitz, J. J. Electro-dynamic field theory in psychiatry. S. *Med. J.,* 1953, 46: 650-660.

16. Ravitz, L. J. Comparative clinical and electro-cyclic observations on twin brothers concordant as to schizophrenia, with periodic manifestations of *folie à deux* phenomena. *J. Nerv. Ment. Dis.,* 1955, 121: 72-87.

17. Ravitz, L. J. Correlation between DC voltage gradients and clinical changes in a chronic schizophrenic patient, project M-223 (film). Abstracted in *The Scientific Papers of the 112th Annual Meeting of the American Psychiatric Association in Summary Form*: 28-C-4. American Psychiatric Association, Washington, D.C., 1956. Selected frames and commentary to be published.

18. Ravitz, L. J., and Cuadra, C. A. Phylogenetic and electro-cyclic implications of schizophrenic states. *Ibid.,* 53. Complete text to be published.

19. Ravitz, L. J. Application of the electro-dynamic field theory in biology, psychiatry, medicine, and hypnosis. I. General survey. *Am. J. Clin. Hyp.,* 1959, 1: 135-150.

20. Ravitz, L. J. History, measurement, and applicability of periodic changes in the electro-magnetic field in health and disease. In *Rhythmic functions in the living system. Annals N.Y. Acad. Scs.,* 1962, 98: 1144-1201.

21. Ravitz, L. J. The danger of scientific prejudice. *Am. J. Clin. Hyp.,* 1968, 10: 282-303.

22. Russell, E. W. The discoveries of Burr and Ravitz: A new way to test personnel. *The Pentagon Seminar 'Techniques of Personnel Assessment'*, L. Meriden Ehrmann, Ed., 1968, 121-125. Washington, D.C.: Office of the Secretary of Defense.

23. Russell, E. W. *Design for Destiny*. London: Neville Spearman Ltd., 1971.

TREE POTENTIALS AND EXTERNAL
FACTORS

Ralph Markson, M.A.

Following is a shortened version of the original work which was the author's Master's Thesis in the Meteorology Department at Pennsylvania State University in 1967.

1

In 1966-1967 the writer undertook a study of whether the geophysical environment is correlated with the electric potential in one form of living system, a tree.

Burr had shown that the electric field of living systems is related to their biological activity and presented evidence that indicated bioelectric fields to be a fundamental property of such systems. With over 20 years of electrical potential measurements made in trees, however, he was unable to associate specific environmental factors with tree potentials. Systematic variations related to temperature, humidity, pressure, rainfall, and illumination were not evident in his record, although diurnal, seasonal, and possibly monthly cycles could be seen.

It was suggested by Burr that the moon's synodic period as well as the 11-year sun-spot cycle could be detected. But more rigorous analysis of the data was needed in order to determine if the geophysical environment was in fact influencing tree potentials.

Burr supplied his complete records for this purpose. They were in the form of tabulated hourly values for two trees during the period 1953 through 1961. Subsequent data have not been reduced but are available in the form of charts from a graphical recorder. These records are continuous up to date and contain air

166

and earth electrical potentials as well as those of two trees on the same time scale. Future research should utilize these later data.

2

There are two possible sources of variation in the relatively steady electric potential in a living system; internal and external. Some of the endogenous forces are well known. Brain waves, heart waves, and the electrical correlates of nerve-muscle preparations all show changes in electric potential associated with biological activity of the system. In general, such measurements can be made under essentially standardized conditions to preclude the influence of relatively slow changing environmental factors. Since variations in continuous recordings of the endogenous parameters are of short duration relative to the rate of environmental changes, adequate control of the experiment is possible.

It is known that factors such as barometric pressure, heat, humidity, and light will influence these measurements. Probably electro-magnetic radiation, cosmic rays, geomagnetism, and the electrical characteristics of the atmosphere will do this also to varying degrees. Control of all possible exogenous factors would be extremely complicated, if not impossible.

In lieu of rigorously controlled laboratory experiments, Burr took another approach. He chose a living system from which continuous records could be obtained for many years. A large old tree was ideal for this, in that the application of electrodes would cause a minimum of disturbance of its normal functioning.* Also it was expected that the tree would continue to live for a long time, providing the same source for the measurement of an electric potential difference.

Simultaneous records of temperature, humidity, barometric

---

* Two electrodes were placed in the tree trunk at heights of 1 and 4 feet from the ground. The upper one was connected to the positive terminal of the voltmeter and the lower one to the negative terminal and grounded. The electrodes were inserted through holes in the bark in contact with the undisturbed cambium.

167

pressure, sunlight, weather conditions, atmospheric potential gradient, earth potential gradient, and cosmic rays were expected to provide a basis for correlations with tree potentials. Over a long period of time, it was reasoned, the external factor or factors, that caused changes in the tree potential, would become evident.

Burr thus instrumented two trees, a maple and an elm, on his estate in Old Lyme, Connecticut, starting in 1943. These provided continuous records (except for brief equipment malfunctions). However, one of the trees died in 1966. In addition, during the early phases of this work, a maple tree was simultaneously measured in New Haven, Connecticut, and provided a basis for comparison between trees 40 miles apart.

Besides the tree potentials, Burr measured temperature, humidity, barometric pressure, and estimated cloudiness and weather. He could find no relationship between the common meteorological factors and tree potentials. The one exception was the passage of some thunderstorms, when tree potentials exhibited anomalous behaviour.* Simultaneous measurements between two electrodes in the earth showed parallel anomalies, except the earth potential graphical trace is 'noisy' for several hours before passage of a squall line and quiet afterwards.

If more commonly considered meteorological variables did not correlate with fluctuations in tree potential, Burr reasoned, one should look at other environmental factors such as atmospheric electricity and possibly cosmic influences such as gravitational tides, solar activity, and cosmic radiation. Accordingly, he installed equipment to measure the potential between electrodes in the earth (about 10 metres apart) and the potential gradient of the air (using the standard electrometer-polonium probe instrument).

It was found that the air and earth potentials fluctuated exactly in phase with the tree potentials. However, sometimes only one (either one) of the trees would fluctuate. No explanation

---

* This may have been due to the tree going into corona and a voltage drop occurring between the electrodes. Such an effect was demonstrated by the author working at the Langmuir Laboratory, Socorro, New Mexico, during the summer of 1965.

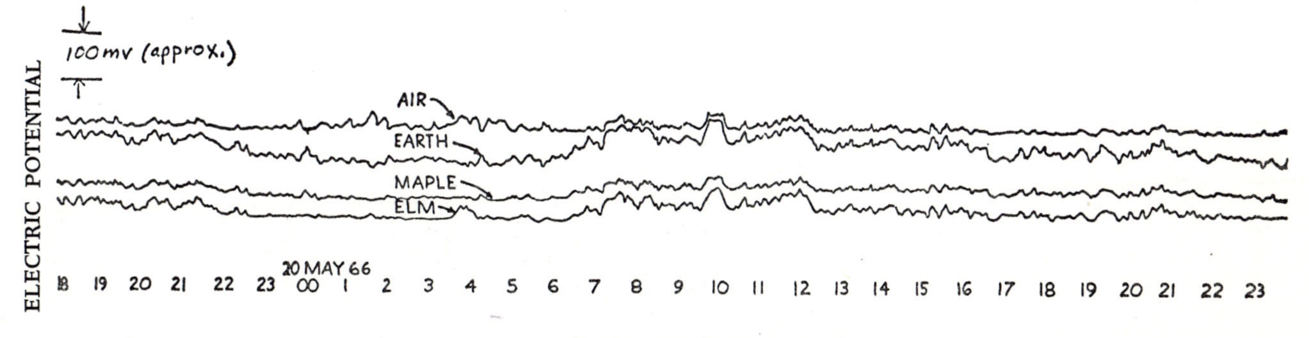

Figure 1. A typical days record of electrical potential difference in the air, earth, maple tree, and elm tree.

is available for this behaviour which remains one of the intriguing questions emerging from Burr's data. Sometimes the air and earth potentials temporarily go 180 degrees out of phase with each other. Examples of these can be seen in Figure 1.

In summary, it is seen that the *electrical environment* correlates with tree potentials while the more obvious meteorological parameters such as light, temperature, and pressure do not in any immediate sense.

3

The absolute range of Burr's tree potentials is 0 to 500 millivolts. Sign is arbitrary and defined initially by Burr making the upper electrode positive. Polarity can reverse with changes in season or large perturbations in potential. Typical values until 1963 were 20 to 100 mv, and subsequently 200 to 400 mv. The reason for this increase is unknown.

The most obvious characteristic of tree potential records is a diurnal cycle, easily seen by inspection. This cycle is typically a minimum in the early morning hours and a maximum during the afternoon. It may vary in magnitude and in phase from day to day, while larger magnitude and phase differences are apparent from season to season.

The range of diurnal variation of tree potentials during the winter months is two or three times that of the summer. The magnitude of tree potentials shows a yearly cycle, a minimum in April, a maximum in September (see Figure 2). In considering the significance of maxima and minima it is necessary to recall that the upper electrode was arbitrarily assigned to be positive. So in essence the seasonal (yearly) cycle shows two inflection points around the time of the equinoxes.

Burr believed he could detect a monthly periodicity in tree potentials related to phase of the moon. Confirmation of the validity of this finding awaited more extensive statistical analysis which will be discussed later in this report.

Analysis of all reduced data (a 15-year period) suggests that the tree potentials are in phase with the sunspot cycle (see Figure 3).

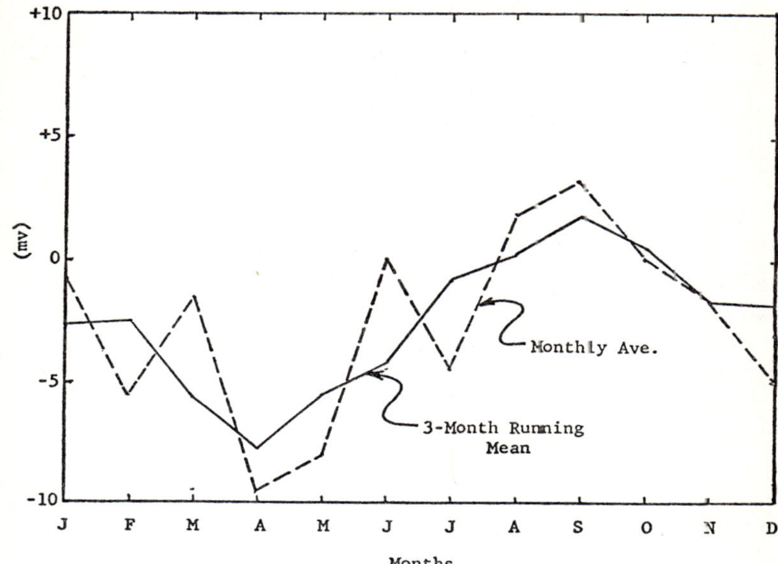

Figure 2. Tree potential monthly averages (1946-1961).

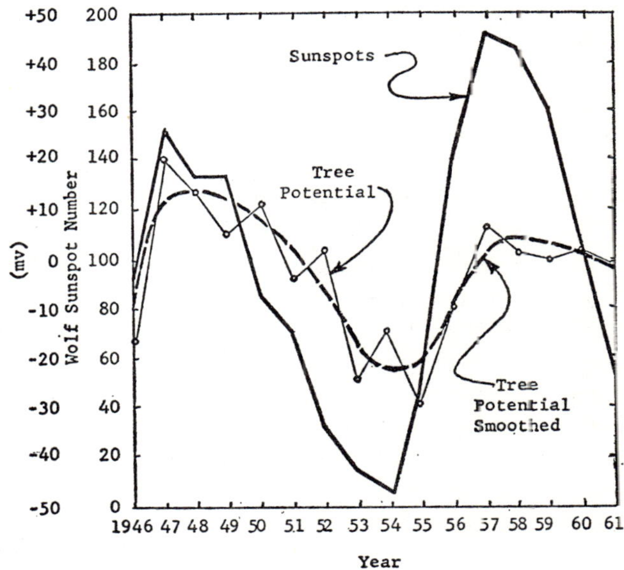

Figure 3. Yearly average tree potentials and sunspot numbers.

171

Since one sunspot cycle lasts about 11 years a longer time series is necessary to establish the relationship more firmly. To investigate the possible importance of solar activity it was decided to check the geomagnetic activity index against tree potentials. This analysis will be described.

As noted above, during the early phases of his work, Burr simultaneously measured two trees which were 40 miles apart. Similarities in these records suggest that they were responding to the same external force which was not local in nature.

Besides the diurnal variation, the other easily seen characteristic in Burr's tree potential records occurs during the period approximately from 10 p.m. to midnight until dawn, when there is little variation (noise) in the record. Around dawn the noise increases and continues until after sunset. The exact onset and termination of the noisier period varies, and on some days this effect is absent. There is no immediate explanation for the phenomenon; it is not dependent on light or noise in the power-lines.

A day's record of tree potentials illustrating the midnight-till-dawn quiet period and typical characteristics of such records was seen in Figure 1.

4

Burr's work showed that the electric field of biological systems was a sensitive indicator of biological activity. There were indications that in some applications the electric field would be used to predict biological activity before it happened. This was evidence for the hypothesis that the electric field of a living system regulated its structure and functioning.

The question then remained as to which factors in the environment might modulate the electric field of living systems. The commonly considered environmental parameters were found not to have immediate influence, although they probably would on a long-term basis, perhaps accounting (at least in part) for the observed seasonal variations. However, less obvious environmental factors, the electric fields in the atmosphere and earth, did correlate with tree potentials and thus may influence biological activity.

Burr also found indications that the moon's position and solar activity influenced tree potentials. This may possibly occur through their modulation of the electro-magnetic environment.

The use of the earth's magnetic field as a geophysical parameter was suggested by the possibility that the magnitude of tree potentials fluctuated with the 11-year sunspot cycle. The geomagnetic field which undergoes variations following solar eruptions provides the best long-term quantitative data for solar-terrestrial research.

The earth's magnetic field is continuously recorded at many observatories throughout the world. Arbitrary scales have been developed to express quantitatively fluctuations in the strength and direction of the magnetic field. In the late 1930s, Bartels developed the A and K indices which have subsequently been used throughout the world. These had the advantage over the previous system of being objectively determined. The A index is first obtained using linear measures of the magnitude and variations of the graphic records. This is transformed to the K index through an arbitrarily defined quasilogarithmic relationship. The range of the A index is 0 to 400 while the range of the K index is 0 to 9. The conversion table is given below.

K	0	1	2	3	4	5	6	7	8	9
A	0	4	7	15	27	48	80	140	240	400

Certain magnetic observatories report their eight daily values, one each for 3-hour periods, which are averaged to determine the planetary magnetic indices Ap and Kp. Normalizing factors are applied to each observatory since magnetic fluctuations are greater near the auroral zones. In investigating the possible relationship of tree potentials to geomagnetic activity, it was decided to use the Ap index because it is a linear measure and does not overly weigh the weaker disturbances.

The technique of superposed-epoch analysis—sometimes simply called 'epoch analysis'—was utilized to see if geomagnetic activity was associated with fluctuations in tree potential. Values of tree potential were tabulated for six days before to six days after specific 'key days'. This 13-day span constitutes an epoch.

Key days were chosen with no advance knowledge of tree potentials by scanning daily Ap values. When a day was found in which the index rose sharply to values at least twice as high as previously—after periods of at least a week when the index was relatively low and steady—such days were designated as key days. During solar minimum the low and steady periods had Ap values below 10, while near solar maximum low and steady Ap values were about 15. Calling the key day the nth day, averages were obtained of the tree potential values for each day from the $n-6$th to the $n+6$th. This analysis was done separately for each year studied. Approximately 20 key days per year were chosen for the years 1953, 1955, 1957, 1959, and 1961. These years span one sunspot cycle from minimum to minimum.

Because the magnitude and variation of tree potentials change for different seasons and years, it was necessary to normalize this parameter. The original tree potentials were tabulated in 24-hourly readings per day. Only the midnight values were used as representative of each day, because this was a time of minimum 'noise' as seen in Figure 1.

If solar activity, as manifest by the magnetic index, is related to tree potentials, one might expect to find anomalous tree potentials on the key days, or afterward if there was a lag in the tree's response. The basic question one must ask in this form of analysis is, 'How do you know an anomalous value of tree potential on a particular day is associated with magnetic activity?' A causal relationship between magnetic activity and tree potential certainly cannot be implied if an abnormal fluctuation in tree potential occurs *before* a solar outburst. However, even if a statistical correlation were found, it would not necessarily imply causality; both parameters could be controlled by some other variable(s).

5

In order to formulate a reasonable hypothesis to test with epoch analysis, it is necessary to consider how solar activity modulates the earth's magnetic field. The sunspot index (Wolf Number) is a crude measure of solar activity, determined simply from the number and grouping of visually observed sunspots. Areas of large sunspots often produce strong solar flares; but flares can also occur in solar regions without sunspots.

Solar flares produce ultraviolet radiation and sometimes x-rays and high-energy cosmic rays. These forms of radiation propagate at or near the speed of light reaching the earth in about eight to fifteen minutes, where they cause ionization and electric currents in the ionosphere. In turn the ionospheric disturbances cause variations in the magnetic field which, when strong enough, are called 'magnetic storms'.

Flares also produce corpuscular radiation particles which propagate more slowly, reaching the earth in about one or two days. When these charged particles hit the upper atmosphere, they also produce ionization. Some are trapped in the magnetosphere, where they are temporarily stored. When sufficiently accelerated in the magnetosphere, they may penetrate deep enough into the atmosphere to cause auroras. Perturbations of the earth's magnetic field are associated with these events.

Thus magnetic storms occur at two times: (1) Immediately after a solar flare—due to wave radiation, and (2) Some time after the solar flare (generally two to four days)—due to corpuscular radiation.

Although it is known that solar particles take about two days to reach the earth and magnetic storms often commence at that time, R. Reiter* has found that the Kp index becomes a maximum on the fourth day following a solar flare. Magnetic storms generally last several days and should not be considered as single events. Additional bundles of solar particles may reach the upper

* Reiter, Reinhold. Relationships between atmospheric electrical phenomena and simultaneous meteorological conditions, *Air Force Cambridge Research Lab.* No. 415, Vol. 1, 169-171, 1960.

atmosphere over a period of several days following a solar eruption. Thus the magnetic disturbance is perpetuated with one magnetic storm superimposed upon the next. The total period of enhanced magnetic activity is typically two or three days and sometimes longer. Therefore, a lag of four days between solar flares and maximum of the magnetic index is not inconsistent with the model.

We can therefore answer the question of what day or days in an epoch might display anomalous tree potentials if they are associated with magnetic activity. Assuming little or no delay in the response of the tree itself, the maximum deviation of tree potentials should occur on the key day which was chosen as having a large increase in magnetic index. Some of these days would correspond to the class of magnetic storms caused by wave radiation and occur shortly after a flare.

According to Reiter's results one would also expect a secondary peak in the tree potential curve on the (n + 4)th day. The nth-day (key day) effect should be strongest as *all* these days have magnetic storms, while the (n + 4)th-day effect should be weaker not being precisely timed, i.e., there is an enhanced probability of magnetic activity on the (n + 4)th day, but only *some* of these days would actually have magnetic storms.

Figure 4 is the result of the five years studied covering one sunspot cycle and a total of 100 epochs. The maximum tree potential variation occurs on the key day. It exceeds the average by 2·3 standard deviations (the 98% confidence level).

A secondary peak of about 1 standard deviation occurs on the (n + 4)th day. While not statistically significant, this is the only other maximum in the curve. Both maxima occur on the two days postulated in the original hypothesis to fit the model.

We can conclude from the result of this analysis that tree potentials respond either to geomagnetic activity directly, or that both parameters may be under the influence of some other geophysical factor or factors.

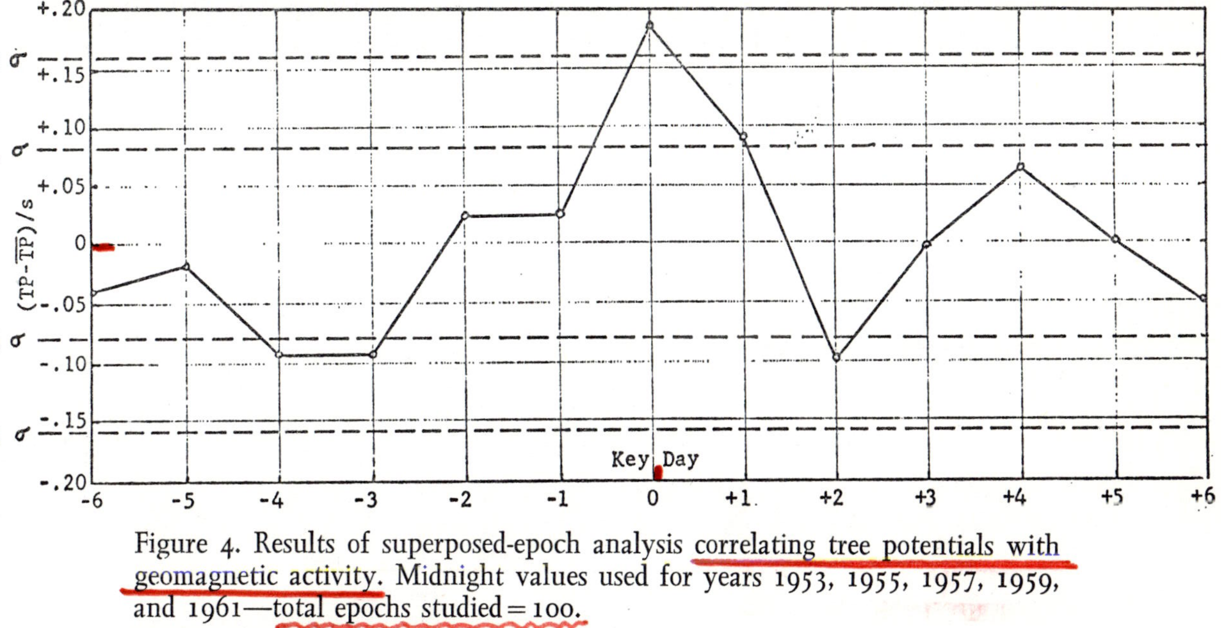

Figure 4. Results of superposed-epoch analysis correlating tree potentials with geomagnetic activity. Midnight values used for years 1953, 1955, 1957, 1959, and 1961—total epochs studied = 100.

$(TP-\overline{TP})/s$ — Normalized Tree Potential Variation.

TP = Midnight tree potential   s = Standard deviation of each epoch
$\overline{TP}$ = Monthly mean of TP   σ = Standard deviation of this curve

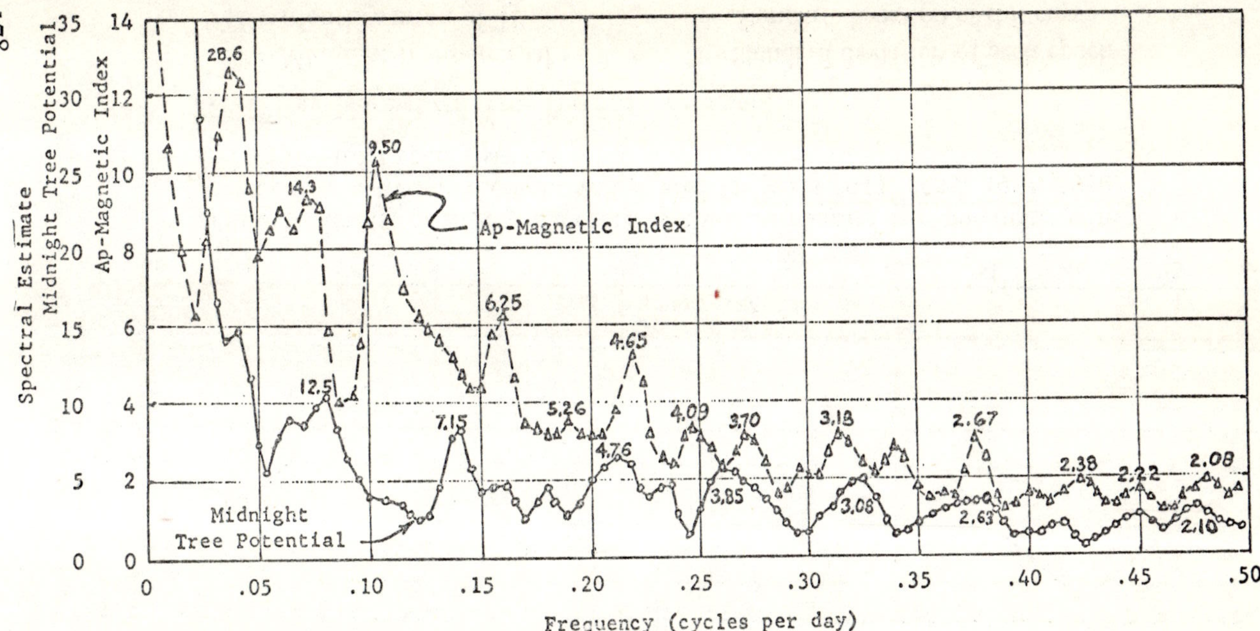

Figure 5. Ap-magnetic index and midnight-tree-potential spectra. January 1953 through December 1960 (2922 days, 100 lags). Numbers at peaks are period of harmonics in days.

6

In order to test for possible periodicities in the tree potential records that could be attributed to the solar-activity period of 27·3 days or to the lunar synodic period of 29·5 days, spectrum analysis was utilized, with the aid of the IBM 7074 computer at the Pennsylvania State University.

Such analysis would indicate what periodicities, if any, were present in the tree potential. Both solar and lunar influences had been suggested by Burr in his earlier work; spectrum analysis might bring out the relative importance of each, and possibly other, environmental influences.

Two time series were utilized; tree potentials at midnight and tree-potential changes at dusk for 2922 days starting with the year 1953. While no periodicity was found in the dusk tree potential changes, significant periodicity appeared in the midnight tree potentials. Figure 5 shows the Ap index and midnight tree potential spectra. The 27-day sunspot period is clearly seen in the former but is not present in the latter. Coherence between the spectra is small and not significant. This does not mean that there is no relationship between the magnetic index and midnight tree potentials. Because the relationship between magnetic storms and tree potentials is probably much weaker than the relationship between sunspot position and magnetic storms, which is weak to start with, it would be expected that little coherence would exist in cross-spectrum analysis between the Ap index and midnight tree-potential spectra. For this reason, according to Brier,* the superposed-epoch analysis is superior to spectrum analysis in bringing out weak relationships.

The midnight tree-potential spectrum shows peaks with periods of: 12·5, 7·15, 4·76, 3·85, 3·08, 2·63, and 2·10 days. This suggested that the peaks were the 2nd, 4th, 6th, 8th, 10th, 12th, and 14th harmonics of a fundamental frequency near 27·3 or 29·5 days (sunspot repetition or lunar synodic periods). Multiply-

* Brier, Glenn. Statistics section, U.S. Weather Bureau. personal communication.

ing each peak period by its corresponding harmonic and taking the mean, we find 29·5 days, the synodic period of the moon.

The question arises as to whether these peaks are really harmonics of some fundamental frequency. If so, a plot of the peak frequency as ordinate against the harmonic as abscissa would result in a straight line. Figure 6 shows such a plot which is close to a straight line. The slope of the solid line, which fits the data well, would be for the moon's synodic period of 29·5 days. The dashed line was drawn by fitting the points using the method of least squares and gives a period of 30·3 days, close to the lunar synodic period. The sunspot period is represented by the dotted line and is well beyond the range of deviation of data points from the line of best fit. This analysis points to the moon and not the sun as influencing tree potentials.

It is important to note that the fundamental period of the moon is not present in the midnight tree-potential spectrum; only the even harmonics are seen. This means the basic frequency is really 14.75 days or half the synodic period; implying a semi-monthly tidal mechanism. The same period was found by Brier and Bradley* in their researches on lunar control of rainfall and is also seen in ocean and atmospheric tides.

The tree-potential spectrum suggests a lunar gravitational mechanism occurring twice a month when the moon is in conjunction and opposition with the sun. It is possible that the moon is not directly influencing the tree potential with its gravitational field but through the electro-magnetic environment which is modulated by the tidal period.

Statistically, both the sun and the moon seem to influence tree potentials, the sun apparently through an electro-magnetic mechanism, the moon through a gravitational or gravitational-electrical mechanism. The moon's effect is more easily detected. It is possible that the lunar effect is not a gravitational one 'per se', but one of modulation of the tree's electro-magnetic environment.

* Brier, G., and Bradley, D. A. The lunar synodical period and precipitation in the United States, *J. Atmos. Sci.*, 21, 386-395, 1964.

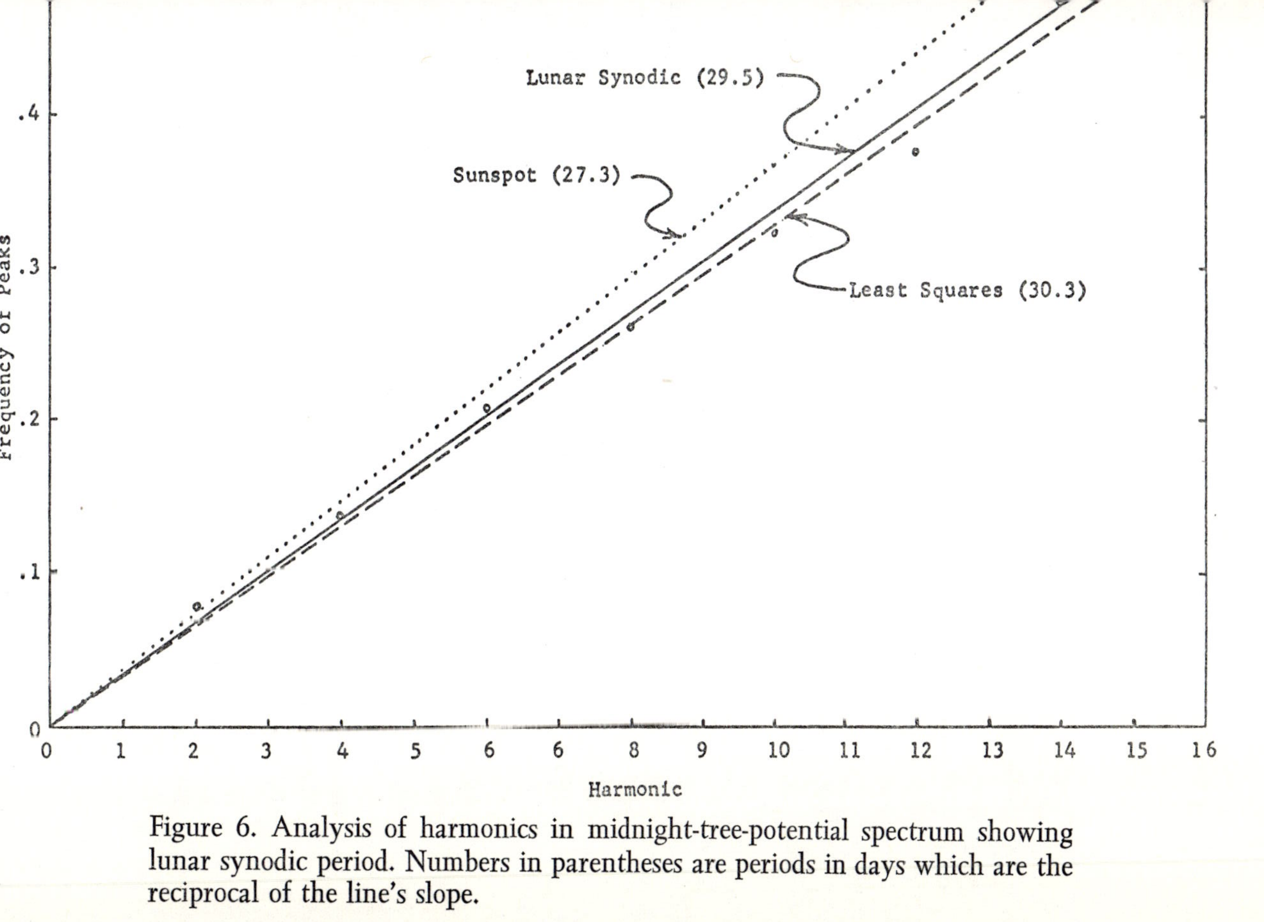

Figure 6. Analysis of harmonics in midnight-tree-potential spectrum showing lunar synodic period. Numbers in parentheses are periods in days which are the reciprocal of the line's slope.

7

This study has suggested further researches that could usefully be pursued in the future:

Superposed-epoch analyses suggested response of tree potentials to rapid increases in the magnetic index. In future research, the validity of this finding could be checked by utilizing the unanalysed data for 1954, 1956, 1958, and 1960.

The exact period present could also be obtained by superposed-epoch analysis, using a modified technique such as Brier's in establishing the lunar periodicity in rainfall. The advantage of the technique is that it makes possible high resolution of periodicities in a time series with only one value per day.

Spectrum analysis utilizing but one value per day and limited to a maximum lag of 100 cannot pinpoint the exact period by means of hourly values (which are available). If the tree potential spectrum could be examined in high resolution for the range between 27- and 30-day periods the exact period could be determined.

Prior to 1962, Burr's data are available only in tabulated form with hourly values. From 1962 through 1966, the original records are available. One typical day is seen in Figure 1. Evaluation of these records would allow for better statistical analysis. They show restlessness in the trace as well as discontinuous changes in mean tree potential. These transients may illustrate basic behaviour of tree potentials, and may lead to an understanding of the mechanisms by which tree potentials respond to the environment.

The signal-to-noise ratio in these data is much higher than in the earlier records. For some unknown reason, around 1963 typical absolute magnitudes increased from below 100 mv. to 200-400 mv., which may allow environmental influences to be isolated that were previously undetectable.

The typical tree potential records contain 'quiet time' periods between about midnight and dawn. Some days do not display this characteristic, and the onset and termination of this period is

182

variable. In the future, it would be of interest to analyse this phenomenon in relation to meteorological, geophysical, and seasonal variables.

Inspection of the later records clearly shows that tree potentials, air potential, and earth potential are generally exactly in phase. However, sometimes only one tree responds or the air and earth potentials go to 180 degrees out of phase. Analysis in regard to the meteorological-geophysical environment may explain these phenomena.

In 1966, the maple tree which provided the records used in this analysis was dying. Finally it had to be cut down. Continuous records are available for this tree from 1962 on. Simultaneous records are available for an elm tree which stood next to the maple. It was noted that the magnitude of electrical potential in the maple tree when it was dying remained the same as before, but the characteristic fluctuations in the record (see Figure 1) became much smaller or ceased, while the healthy elm tree displayed its normal fluctuations in phase or out of phase with the air and earth potentials. This interesting phenomenon should be analysed.

The effect of imposing electric, magnetic, and electro-magnetic radiation fields on the electrical potential of living systems can be studied in the laboratory, with fields of the order of those occurring naturally. Animals and plants might be studied simultaneously in order to determine whether or not different living systems respond simultaneously to changes in the electro-magnetic environment. Also, if electrical potential is a function of the state of health one would expect to see characteristic differences in the electrical records of disturbed, sick, or dying systems. Such responses might eventually serve as a diagnostic tool.

If the electric field of living systems is an indicator of biological activity and possibly a regulator of it, then geophysical factors may be of extreme importance for men venturing into space, so that measurements of their electrical potential, along with other biomedical parameters, might well have to be considered. Such information may provide the answer to how man's geophysical environment affects him and may give clues to the classical mystery of biological clocks. The understanding and use of electrical potentials in living systems may be an important part of the new 'space age' science of exobiology.

APPENDIX

BIBLIOGRAPHY OF
HAROLD SAXTON BURR

1916
1. The effects of the removal of the nasal pits in Amblystoma embryos. *J. exp. Zool.*, 1916, 20: 2757.
2. Regeneration in the brain of Amblystoma. *J. comp. Neurol.*, 1916, 26: 203-211.

1918
3. Breeding habits, maturation of eggs and ovulation of the albino rat. *Amer. J. Anat.*, 1918, 15: 291-317.

1920
4. The transplantation of the cerebral hemispheres of Amblystoma. *J. exp. Zool.*, 1920, 30: 159-169.

1922
5. The early development of the cerebral hemispheres in Amblystoma. *J. comp. Neurol.*, 1922, 34: 277-301.

1924
6. An experimental study of the origin of the meninges. *Proc. Soc. exp. Biol.* (N.Y.), 1924, 22: 52-53 (with S. C. Harvey).
7. Some experiments on the transplantation of the olfactory placode in Amblystoma. 1. An experimentally produced aberrant cranial nerve. *J. comp. Neurol.*, 1924, 37: 455-479.

1925
8. An anatomical study of the gasserian ganglion, with particular refrence to the nature and extent of Meckel's cave. *Anat. Rec.*, 1925, 29: 269-289 (with G. B. Robinson).

1926

9. An experimental study of the action of hyoscine hydrobromide on the nervous system of Amblystoma. *J. comp. Neurol.*, 1926, 41: 401-421.
10. The development of the meninges. *Arch. Neurol. Psychiat.*, 1926, 15: 545-565 (with S. C. Harvey).

1928

11. Certain factors determining the direction of growth of nerve fibres. *Science*, 1928, 74: 604.
12. The central nervous system of Orthagoriscus mola. *J. comp. Neurol.*, 1928, 45: 33-128.

1929

13. Jonathan Knight and the founding of the Yale Medical School. *Yale J. Biol. Med.*, 1929, 1: 327-343.

1930

14. Hyperplasia in the brain of Amblystoma. *J. exp. Zool.*, 1930, 55: 171-191.
15. Disciplines. *Yale J. Biol. Med.*, 1930, 3: 151-157.

1931

16. The preclinical sciences and human biology. *Yale J. Biol. Med.*, 1931, 4: 63-68.
17. Development of the meninges in the chick. *Proc. Soc. exp. Biol. (N.Y.)*, 1931, 28: 974-976 (with S. C. Harvey).

1932

18. Determinants of organization in the cerebral hemispheres. *Res. Publ. Ass. nerv. ment. Dis.*, 1932, 13: 39-48.
19. An electro-dynamic theory of development suggested by studies of proliferation rates in the brain of Amblystoma. *J. comp. Neurol.*, 1932, 56: 347-371.

1933

20. Development of the meninges. *Arch. Neurol. Psychiat.*, 1933, 29: 683-690 (with S. C. Harvey).

APPENDIX

1934

21. The founding of the Medical Institution of Yale College. *Yale J. Biol. Med.*, 1934, 6: 333-340.
22. Some observations on the neural mechanisms of Opistho-proctus Soleatus Vaillant. *Psychiat. neurol. Bl.*, 1934, 38: 407-416 (with G. M. Smith).
23. Sympathetic components of the genito-femoral and obturator nerves in the Rhesus monkey (Macaca mulatta). *Anat. Rec.*, 1934, 61: 53-56 (with S. Zuckerman).

1935

24. A study of the effects of intermedin and injury of the hypophysis on traumatic corial melanophores in goldfishes. *Endocrinology*, 1935, 19: 409-412 (with G. M. Smith and R. S. Ferguson).
25. The electro-dynamic theory of life. *Quart. Rev. Biol.*, 1935, 10: 322-333 (with F. S. C. Northrop).
26. Electrical characteristics of living systems. *Yale J. Biol. Med.*, 1935, 8: 31-35 (with C. T. Lane).
27. Detection of ovulation in the intact rabbit. *Proc. Soc. exp. Biol.* (N.Y.), 1935, 33: 109-111 (with R. T. Hill and Edgar Allen).

1936

28. Electro-dynamic studies of mice with developing cancer of the mammary gland. *Anat. Rec.*, 1936, 64: 7-8.
29. A vacuum tube microvoltmeter for the measurement of bio-electric phenomena. *Yale J. Biol. Med.*, 1936, 9: 65-76 (with C. T. Lane and L. F. Nims).
30. Bio-electric phenomena associated with menstruation. *Yale J. Biol. Med.*, 1936, 9: 155-158 (with L. K. Musselman).

1937

31. Experimental findings concerning the electro-dynamic theory of life and an analysis of their physical meaning. *Growth*, 1937, 1: 78-88 (with F. S. C. Northrop).
32. Bio-electric potential gradients in the chick. *Yale J. Biol. Med.*, 1937, 9: 247-258 (with C. I. Hovland).

33. Bio-electric correlates of development in Amblystoma. *Yale J. Biol. Med.*, 1937, 9: 541-549 (with C. I. Hovland).
34. Medical fees in the colonial period. *Yale J. Biol. Med.*, 1937, 9: 359-364.
35. A bio-electric record of human ovulation. *Science*, 1937, 86: 312 (with L. K. Musselman, D. Barton, and N. Kelley).
36. Bio-electric correlates of human ovulation. *Yale J. Biol. Med.*, 1937, 10: 155-160 (with L. K. Musselman, D. Barton, and N. Kelley).

1938

37. Steady-state electrical properties of the human organism during sleep. *Yale J. Biol. Med.*, 1938, 10: 271-274 (with D. S. Barton).
38. Bio-electric properties of cancer-resistant and cancer-susceptible mice. *Amer. J. Cancer*, 1938, 32: 240-248 (with L. C. Strong and G. M. Smith).
39. Bio-electric correlates of the menstrual cycle in women. *Amer. J. Obstet. Gynec.*, 1938, 35: 743-751 (with L. K. Musselman).
40. Bio-electric correlates of methylcolanthrene-induced tumours in mice. *Yale J. Biol. Med.*, 1938, 10: 539-544 (with L. C. Strong and G. M. Smith).
41. The relationship between the bio-electric potential of rats and certain drugs. *Yale J. Biol. Med.*, 1938, 11: 137-140 (with P. K. Smith).
42. The measurement of pH in circulating blood. *Science*, 1938, 87: 197-198 (with L. F. Nims and Clyde Marshall).
43. Bio-electric correlates of wound healing. *Yale J. Biol. Med.*, 1938, 11: 104-107 (with S. C. Harvey and Max Taffel).

1939

44. Evidence for the existence of an electro-dynamic field in living organisms. *Proc. nat. Acad. Sci.*, 1939, 25: 284-288 (with F. S. C. Northrop).
45. A preliminary study of electrical correlates of growth in Obelia geniculata. *Growth*, 1939, 3: 211-220 (with Fred S. Hammett).

46. Voltage gradients in the nervous system. *Trans. Amer. neurol. Ass.*, 1939, 65: 11-14 (with P. J. Harman, Jr.).
47. Vocationalism in the university. *Yale J. Biol. Med.*, 1939, 12: 199-204.
48. Animal electricity. *Yale scient. Mag.*, 1939, 13: 5.

1940

49. Biologic organization and the cancer problem. *Yale J. Biol. Med.*, 1940, 12: 277-282.
50. Vaginal electrical correlates of the estrous cycle of the rat. *Anat. Rec.*, 1954, 76: 8 (with John Boling and D. Barton).
51. An electro-metric study of the healing wound in man. *Yale J. Biol. Med.*, 1940, 12: 483-485 (with Max Taffel and S. C. Harvey).
52. Harry Burr Ferris. *Science*, 1940, 92: 499-500.
53. Electro-metric studies of tumours induced in mice by the external application of benzpyrene. *Yale J. Biol. Med.*, 1940, 12: 711-717 (with G. M. Smith and L. C. Strong).

1941

54. Factors associated with vaginal electrical correlates of the estrous cycle of the albino rat. *Anat. Rec.*, 1941, 79: 9 (with John Boling).
55. Field properties of the developing frog's egg. *Proc. nat. Acad. Sci.*, 1941, 27: 276-281.
56. Changes in the field properties of mice with transplanted tumours. *Yale J. Biol. Med.*, 1941, 13: 783-788.
57. An electro-metric study of uterine activity. *Amer. J. Obstet. Gynec.*, 1941, 42: 59-67 (with L. Langman).
58. Steady state potential differences in the early development of Amblystoma. *Yale J. Biol. Med.*, 1941, 14: 51-57 (with T. H. Bullock).

1942

59. An electrical study of the human cervix uteri. *Anat. Rec.*, 1942, 82: 35-36 (with L. Langman).
60. Electrical correlates of growth in corn roots. *Yale J. Biol. Med.*, 1942, 14: 581-588.

APPENDIX

61. Electro-metric timing of human ovulation. *Amer. J. Obstet. Gynec.*, 1942, 44: 223-230 (with L. Langman).

1943

62. Neuroid transmission in mimosa. *Anat. Rec.*, 1943, 85: 12.
63. Electrical correlates of pure and hybrid strains of corn. *Proc. nat. Acad. Sci.*, 1943, 29: 163-166.
64. Electrical polarization of pacemaker neurons. *J. Neurophysiol.*, 1943, 6: 85-97 (with T. H. Bullock).
65. An electro-metric study of mimosa. *Yale J. Biol. Med.*, 1943, 15: 823-829.

1944

66. Moon-madness. *Yale J. Biol. Med.*, 1944, 16: 249-256.
67. A biologist considers social security. *Conn. St. med. J.*, 1944, 8: 165.
68. Potential gradients in living systems and their measurements. Pp. 1117-1121 in *Medical Physics*. Chicago, The Year Book Publishers, Inc. [c1944].
69. The meaning of bio-electric potentials. *Yale J. Biol. Med.*, 1944, 16: 353-360.
70. Electric correlates of form in Cucurbit fruits. *Amer. J. Botany*, 1944, 31: 249-253 (with E. W. Sinnott).
71. Electricity and life: phases of moon correlated with life cycle. *Yale scient. Mag.*, 1944, 18: 5-6.

1945

72. Variables in DC measurement. *Yale J. Biol. Med.*, 1945, 17: 465-478.
73. Diurnal potentials in the maple tree. *Yale J. Biol. Med.*, 1945, 17: 727-734.

1946

74. Electrical correlates of peripheral nerve injury. A preliminary note. *Science*, 1946, 103: 48-49 (with R. G. Grenell).
75. Growth correlates of electromotive forces in maize seeds. *Proc. nat. Acad. Sci.*, 1946, 32: 73-84 (with Oliver Nelson, Jr.).

76. Surface potentials and peripheral nerve injury: A clinical test. *Yale J. Biol. Med.*, 1946, 18: 517-525 (with R. G. Grenell).

1947

77. Tree potentials. *Yale J. Biol. Med.*, 1947, 19: 311-318.
78. Electro-magnetic studies in women with malignancy of cervix uteri. *Science*, 1947, 105: 209-210 (with L. Langman).
79. Field theory in biology. *Sci. Monthly*, 1947, 64: 217-225.
80. Surface potentials and peripheral nerve regeneration. *Fed. Proc.*, 1947, 6: 117 (with R. G. Grenell).

1948

81. A commentary on full-time teaching. *Conn. St. med. J.*, 1948, 12: 937-940.

1949

82. Millivoltmeters. *Yale J. Biol. Med.*, 1949, 21: 249-253 (with A. Mauro).
83. A technique to aid in the detection of malignancy of the female genital tract. *Amer. J. Obstet. Gynec.*, 1949, 57: 274-281.
84. Electro-static fields of the sciatic nerve in the frog. *Yale J. Biol. Med.*, 1949, 21: 455-462 (with A. Mauro).
85. The Connecticut State Medical Society. *Conn. St. med. J.*, 1949, 13: 950-955.

1950

86. Electro-metric study of cotton seeds. *J. exp. Zool.*, 1950, 113: 201-210.
87. Bioelectricity: potential gradients, Pp. 90-94 in *Medical Physics*. Chicago, The Year Book Publishers, Inc., 1950.

1952

88. Electro-metrics of atypical growth. *Yale J. Biol. Med.*, 1952, 25: 67-75.

APPENDIX

1953
89. Electrical correlates of ovulation in the rhesus monkey. *Yale J. Biol. Med.*, 1953, 25: 408-417 (with V. L. Gott).

1954
90. Confusion or configuration? *The Astronomical League Bulletin*, 1954, 4: No. 4.

1955
91. Certain electrical properties of the slime mould. *J. exp. Zool.*, 1955, 129: 327-342.
92. Response of the slime mould to electric stimulus. *Science*, 1955, 122: 1020-1021 (with William Seifriz).

1956
93. Effect of a severe storm on electric properties of a tree and the earth. *Science*, 1956, 124: 1204-1205.